POEMS FOR A SMALL PLANET

BEN hAS MY COPY Of ANOthER COUNTRY

A BREAD LOAF ANTHOLOGY

The Bread Loaf Anthology of Contemporary American Poetry, edited by Robert Pack, Sydney Lea, and Jay Parini, 1985.

The Bread Loaf Anthology of Contemporary American Short Stories, edited by Robert Pack and Jay Parini, 1987.

The Bread Loaf Anthology of Contemporary American Essays, edited by Robert Pack and Jay Parini, 1989.

Writers on Writing, edited by Robert Pack and Jay Parini, 1991.

Poems for a Small Planet: Contemporary American Nature Poetry edited by Robert Pack and Jay Parini, 1993.

EDITED BY

Robert Pack

Jay Parini

Poems for a Small Planet

Contemporary American Nature Poetry

Middlebury College Press

Published by University Press of New England

Hanover and London

MIDDLEBURY COLLEGE PRESS

Published by University Press of New England, Hanover, NH 03755

Printed in the United States of America 5 4 3 2 1

CIP data appear at the end of the book

Acknowledgments for previously published material appear on p. 301

CONTENTS

JAY PARINI

Introduction

The Chinese poet Ch'en Yu Yi, writing in the fifth century A.D., framed the dilemma of the "nature poet" with typical brevity:

Dawn. Birds sing in the courtyard.
Spring overwhelms the forest
With flowers. All of a sudden
A beautiful poem appears
Before me. When I try to catch
It in the nets of prosody
I can't find them.

(trans. Kenneth Rexroth)

What the poet has seized upon here is the eternal issue of how a poet "catches" nature in the nets of prosody. It raises the further question of what "nature" is, especially in the context of language.

Especially since the dawn of Romanticism, nature has become a central preoccupation of poets. As the intellectual historian A. O. Lovejoy pointed out, "nature" as a term is used by critics and poets alike until after the mid-eighteenth century to refer to two main areas: the human mind and the natural world. In the mind, it is allied with those parts of human perception that are the "most spontaneous, unpremeditated, untouched by reflection or design, and free from the bondage of social convention." With regard to the natural world, it is associated with those parts of the universe "which come into being independently of human effort and contrivance."

Thus Romantic poets from Wordsworth to Goethe went back to nature as a way to escape the highly mechanized, industrialized world that had become the main reality of life. The "dark Satanic mills" that William Blake invoked and disparaged had come to clot the British landscape. Increasingly, nature had been pushed to one side, cordoned off, turned into "parks" and "green belts." The wilderness, in Britain, was pretty much gone by the dawn of the twentieth century, and in America the beginnings of the same process could be seen by the end of the Civil War.

The American response to the Romantic obsession with nature is embodied by Ralph Waldo Emerson, who in his famous essay called *Nature* (1836) declared that "Nature is the symbol of the spirit." Every natural fact was seen by Emerson as reflecting some spiritual fact. The Platonic theory of knowledge that underlies this concept is obvious enough: nature is itself artificial, a reflection of some Ideal form. The Reality behind the physical universe is the spiritual reality. One sees this concept of nature working itself out in the Idealist American poets from Whitman to Roethke and James Wright.

Ironically, it was Henry David Thoreau, the great friend and leading disciple of Emerson, who most firmly plowed the field of American nature writing. Thoreau certainly accepted in theory the Platonism of Emerson, but his mammoth *Journals*—the chief work of his life as a writer—are full of concrete descriptions of natural phenomena that seem to value the natural world for its own sake. He gloried in the details, and he studied them with a sense of calm one associates more with scientific inquiry than prophetic poetry.

In our post-Romantic age, it is no longer possible for poets to "worship nature" in the unironic ways of nineteenth-century poetry. The question now, as Robert Frost put it so poignantly, is "What to make of a diminished thing." We have come to a point where human greed and stupidity have shrunk the natural world in hideous ways. Agricultural land has been destroyed by farming methods that sacrifice irreplaceable topsoil and destroy the quality of the soil that is left with chemicals designed, in the short run, to force production. And wilderness areas have continued to shrink as economic forces push developers and lumber mill operators to utilize this land in destructive ways.

American children now spend their time in air-conditioned malls where "nature" is reduced to a pathetic fountain in the lobby with a few plastic trees "growing" by its side. The federal government is busy trying to sell off wilderness areas, while acid rain is pelting them from above. *The Waste Land*, T. S. Eliot's prophetic poem, has become for most people a boring reality. The Thames that ran so sweetly for the Elizabethan poets, so pollution free, is now full of "empty bottles, sandwich papers, / Silk handkerchiefs, cardboard boxes, cigarette ends" and other debris. Now the wind "crosses the brown," and it reeks of garbage. Helplessly, "the human engine waits / Like a taxi throbbing."

How do poets, then, in this last decade of the twentieth century, respond to the destruction of nature? Is natural imagery still a source of comfort? Are the metaphors that derive from natural processes still relevant? Is the old dilemma of Ch'en Yu Yi still in play? Is there hope for a sane way of life, for something like what used to be called "harmony with nature"? The questions multiply endlessly. Must we suffer the ruin of the planet in silence?

In this anthology we have gathered some recent responses to these questions. The poems are all, implicitly more than explicitly, responses to the ecological crisis, to "nature" in its various manifestations: nature as wilderness, "naturalized" nature, human nature. What we find is that the traditions of nature poetry continue to serve us well, even as we willfully misread them. Poets have taken their Romantic precursors seriously, have swallowed them, digested them, reformulated and contradicted them. Nature is no longer the rustic retreat of the Wordsworthian poet in flight from "false refinements." Nature is now a pressing political question, a question of survival. It is now a concept desperately in need of deconstruction, and a process that must be studied for clues to the nature of human nature itself.

The poetry included here is all recent, and the poets represent a wide range of styles and approaches to the art of poetry. We interpret the term "nature poetry" itself broadly to mean poems that in some way reflect a highly developed consciousness of the natural world. The reader will find poems here that treat the ecological crisis directly, but most of them are indirect. There are poems of praise, poems that celebrate "human" nature, poems that grapple with the eternal issue of natural representation itself—the subject of Ch'en Yu Yi's poem quoted earlier. In an historical Afterword, my coeditor, Robert Pack, offers a reflective overview of the traditions of nature poetry in the West that is designed to put the anthology into a larger context. *Poems for a Small Planet*, as a whole, might be thought of as a defense of nature, a stand against all efforts to diminish what Gerard Manley Hopkins calls "the rise, the roll, the carol of creation."

POEMS FOR A SMALL PLANET

SANDRA ALCOSSER

What Makes the Grizzlies Dance

June and finally the snowpeas
sweeten in the Mission Valley.
High behind the numinous meadows
lady bugs swarm, like huge
lacquered fans from Hong Kong,
like the serrated skirts
of blown poppies,
whole mountains turn red.
And in the blue penstemon
grizzly bears swirl
as they gaily bat the snaps
of color against their ragged mouths.
Have you never wanted to spin like that
on hairy, leathered feet
amid the swelling berries
as you tasted a language
of early summer? Shaping
the lazy operatic vowels,
cracking the hard-shelled
consonants like speckled
insects between your teeth,
have you never wanted
to waltz the hills
like a beast?

Glory Monster

Tipped goblets, the blue herons
flap across the glassy pond.
Two then four, they chase each other,
then stop at the penciled shoreline
to wrap their necks together.

How like you, Iris, twisting
your green stems in the grasses.

Heron flowers, humid and patient as fists
that spring to flying buttresses,
stained cathedral naves—

if I were to make a monster, Iris,
to chase me, to suffocate in its bloom,
it would be you. Here comes Iris
marching across the pasture, waving
her rapier skirt, twirling

her caterpillar furs. Oh sing
of the brevity of life
and the ephemeral nature of pleasure,
erotic and funereal anguish,
dark-rivered nectar.

Once I lay by a bed of iris
and once by my dying father
and each time I pressed my face
against the damp
and shriveling flesh.

Woodpecker

On the day the poppies
burst their tight green fists
and the geum and the geranium
bloomed all bloody red
and ruby, so the pileated woodpecker
returned.

He ricocheted off the pine trunk,
and picking among the yellow bugs
sped quickly to the pea vines.
Fat-breasted, he drilled his name,
then let it drip and trill
round the forest, down his throat,
landlord of the mountain, mafioso
in a tweed vest, red-crested whale
of the sky, he announced
the summer solstice.

And we ran to the window
knowing at last snow would melt
on the Bitterroots to flood our fields,
knowing it was time for aurora borealis,
heaven's beast, her tentacles
flicking like jellyfish on the shortest
night of the year.

And we did the dance of the woodpecker,
the fat flicker, the pagan priest,
when the clover bloomed, the salsify
and wild roses, and we knew
that winter was over, we did the dance
of the smart, hard-headed, flashy
creatures of the world.

After all, in summer when blood is thick
and dark as the flicker's crest, when we might
all fatten on berries and weeds alone,
isn't there room for each of us,
even the greedy ones? After all,
have you never wanted to drive at top speed,
to slam into a tree or dive from a ledge
or catch fire or slit your wrists
and let the fluids geyser?
Not suicide, but its burning,
not rage directed at humankind—
no, the heart remains
a sweet berry and ripe.

But red drives the stickleback wild,
red small spots among the green, amongst
the brown rocks. And so on the long day
of the summer solstice when the world
spins silly with light, we do the dance
of the woodpecker, twirling our skirts
and mustaches, tapping our resonant
branches, our underwear
flashing white as we shake
the irregular flags of our body
into undulant, raw flight.

Approaching August

Night takes on its own elegance.
The catenary curve of snakes,
the breathing, pentagonal-shaped
flowers, the shadblow pliant
and black with berries. Orion
rises in the east, over
fat green gardens, and all meanness
is forgiven.

We canoe the river
in the amethyst hour before dark.
Twenty-five billion beats to each heart.
Two passengers fish, two paddle
past the chalk caves, the banks
of aster, the flood plains dense
with white tail and beaver.

We are lost near midnight, a moonless
summer evening, midseason in our senses,
midlife. The sky overhead like glitter ice.
The water round swollen cottonwoods
pulls like tresses and torn paper.

Today I had a letter from France.
"What a truly civilized nation," my friend wrote
as she drank her morning coffee with thick cream
in a country cafe near Avignon. "To my right
a man in a black tuxedo sips raspberry liqueur
and soda."

And here on the same latitude we lie back at dawn
on the caving bank of the Bitterroot.
A shadow slips through the silver grasses.
And then a moth.
And then the moon.

Golden-Mantled Ground Squirrel

Obsequious squeaker
with a jerked-beef tail
you come begging
outside my screen. Sidelong
you stare all morning.
I know that greeting. It's the same as mine.
You can't make up your flimsy mind.
Do you like the world better—distant
or direct? Little Beckett
shifting chicles from one nervous cheek
to the other, will you never seek more
than safe passage?
If I so much as breathe, you convulse
like water on hot grease. Relax,
no one cares about you. If you left
the territory next Friday for good,
there'd be no party. That's the privilege
of being discreet. You know the warm dens,
the sound of your solitary beat
against the walls, and those strawberries
ripening under my porch,
the ones no hand can reach?
They're yours—
deep maroon, reclusive,
they smell so sweet.

PAMELA ALEXANDER

First Relations

Part of the darkness lived. Furred or scaled
according to its mood, it crawled or bounded, snorted
or drooled, it swam or ripped bark from trees,
and it was powerful because it could do all these things at once
and because it could show itself or transmogrify
into boulder, log, hummock of grass. We gave it our fear
freely and bountifully so it would not take more of us;
we made words and gave it a name we never spoke.
Still it pressed so close we tasted its breath, felt our bones
seized. And so we slept with fire, which we also feared.
Children rose up, blood-hot, hungry. We were many.
Some of us predicted its shapes from clouds, some
studied its scents, some imitated its calls and silences;
and we followed it everywhere, darkness in our hands.

Antichromatic

A few people had gone out to see if the trees
were still there, and they were, which made us feel safe
for a moment. Then they said (panting, because they had hurried)
that the trees were no longer lit by sunlight
on their tops and sides, nor were they green any more.
We knew the animals had left long ago, quietly,
species by species, the way they board the Ark
in the ancient story. What we didn't know, hadn't seen
with our color vision and the convolutions
of our blue-gray brains, was that when the birds left—
the toucans and yellow parrots, the cockatoos
and scissor-tailed fly-catchers—they took the colors.
Of course we should have known, we told each other,
it's reasonable, they had the most to lose. Then
we didn't know what to do.

JULIA ALVAREZ

On a Hill above Your House

Down hill, I see a tangle of lights
populate the dark valley below.
The children's lights have long been out,
and the lovers' yearning hands
have touched the fond, familiar spots
like grazing animals at dusk
returning to the glowing barn.

You sleep below in a darkened house,
while up, mid-night, insomniac,
I wonder which might be your home
among the shadowy clumps below.
A car goes by—an unstrung light
moving along a strip of road.
Above, the mirroring autumn sky
reflects a twinkling neighborhood.

By habit I look up to wish
on the first star that I see.
But when my eye fastens on one
my mind is blank of anything
but the thought of you below
your long lean body limp with sleep.

Cows

Seen from a distance, dappled and picturesque
in the green meadows of June, they are schoolgirls
on a Saturday outing with their doting teacher,
fussing at braid ribbons, sashes, reminding them
where there is mud, where there are briars, thorns.
You expect them to form a single file, uphill
singing their school song. But no,
they do not budge. It's you who climb

over the fence to take a second look.
Now they are matrons, big portly flanks
of settled ideas, how things are done,
rights and wrongs like clunky bells at their necks.
They should be wearing ruffles at those necks,
tight little lace-up boots in all this mud.
They should be having polite conversation,
cliches like dainty china tinkling with use.
Doe eyes turn towards you as you approach
seeing, unseeing, who knows? There is no reaction—
as if you had time-traveled here, a future ghost
among these Victorian ladies at their repose
in these their green, impeccable 19th century parlors.
But look close, the future you dragged here
like mud on your shoes has soiled their thick carpets.
Before your eyes these gals are coming apart:
green cud dribbling from their mouths, udders
distended and pink hang close to the ground,
nipples leaking near to their milking time.
It's as if you were watching their becoming
contemporaries. Down with proprieties!
The ladies grow randy, decadent, belch their moos.
They chew their cud noisily, lift their tails,
and drop their turds, amble away, wagging their hips.
As if the most indentured, settled mind
might break the bonds by which it enslaves itself
climb over the fence to take a closer look.

A. R. AMMONS

Standing Light Up

Thunder grumbles, drops, thuds, breaking
down away (gravel-road rubble) the heads

hidden up in summer haze—and none of the
lightning's veins shows: it could be mountains

lost as much as clouds up there, and the sound
could be of equivalences coming down, avalanches

of stone, mud, snow, not just a front and all-day
soak making up—but so what, anything can be

with a little ink and type produced: take the
truth that in a drizzle drops tickle leaves so

it's a pause whether it's a breeze: who cares
about a truth like that: nearly all, maybe

all, most truth doesn't matter a tittle of rubble
or rain: what matters is that sometimes the

spirit halts and listens for what outleaps
the insides of summits thunder's rumble has

never jarred: what is to be seen within
scares the eye brighter than any lightning.

Looking Way Off

The winter day after days
of lows and flurries,
and one trench of snow,
cleared brilliantly and I

went to the window to see
the sun, striking through
everything from blue spruce
to black rose-branch

to the tops of gold burdock,
touch down on the ridge,
the clarity, the line,
the dazzling dalliance and

surprising myself said,
"Make me right," but tightened
airless till, till I imagined
from on high an unassenting

reply, "You're right wrong."
so I cleave to my holding.

Somers Point

What are you doing out here
this windy on the headland
said the bay reeds bent inland,

their bounding tassels like
blurred drops trying to rain ashore,
the bay water thrashing

to land or get away to the open,
the holly, its held leaves
jangling tambourines, the

whipping cypresses simmering and
seething:
oh I said I've come out here

to hide in the trembling
from my trembling, storm roars
outsounding blood roars, sprints

of pulse surpassed by clacking leaves,
to count how many, many
particulars ease could come into.

First Cold

Well, the white asters
are wide open (there's
even a chicory
blossom or two
left on a big weed)

but it's too cold
for the bees to come:
every now and then
a snowflake
streaks

out of the hanging gray,
winter's very first whitening:
white on white let it be,
then, flake
to petal—to hold for a

minute or so: meanwhile,
golden bees are milling at
the door, to pour
out should that other
gold, the sun, break in.

White Echo

The willow's knotty threads
select scant weave from the flurry,
the threads fluffing up a little

to cotton on one side, but
it's so calm the flakes
barely find a side to come from,

a straight downward mingling
turning around as it sometimes does
midair as if to define

ambient mounds of itself to hold
and keep or come back round to:
it's hard to burden a skinny

willow down with snow—ice
would be a different matter, rain
glazing and freezing swelling

laminations, a holding that could
split the willow's giving, branch-splits
skinning the trunk, could, I hope

it won't, this willow's weeping
so huge a summer somberness—
willow stringknots are fast

leeches (spring changes them into pollen
and leaves), the blunt end attached
to the string, the rest tapering

downward so it won't catch anything
unbearably heavy or only
the fluffiest flake on its hump or, of

course, the microinscriptions of
building rain: (soft, blurry snow
blunders into airy holds): sifted

lightly on one side, though, with
snow, a whole tree-ghost can be
shattered free by a striking gust,

white dust stemless, traveling branchless,
shaken whole off side till a breaking
current collapses the snow willow into willow.

DAVID BAKER

Sex

Such joy
            —abundant, indiscriminate!—
these easy June evenings.

It's the cottonwoods all over town and down
along the bluegill creek swollen
this week by the rains,
                        like a bad ankle . . .

I mean, the cottonwoods all week
flinging their sex outward

and down, all the fluff and detritus of their seeds
swaying and easing

onto the trim yards, the somnolent cars,
settling even into the garden of purest cultivation
—oh fine membrane of desire!—
                        or losing themselves

somewhere into the winds which never seem
quite to let up.

Male or female—the characteristic of the cottonwood
being its unisex flower
and a catkin, a cluster
of seed-bearing spikes—it's just got this news,

this delirious joy,
                and when
all of its joy has been plentifully broadcast,
like some dreamy snow or old money,

it's got this sadness—green and down-leaning—
that only the human could love.

The Yard

Bunchgrass or the months-dry wheat
and blanched-white scuff of blue and zoysia
or, in fists, in stubby tufts among the mulch,
the tubular, shiny wild oniongrass . . .

wherever you look it's green sprouts, leaf-shoots—
wherever you step it's as if newly shod, soft
along the thaw, the edging. If this were anything
but language you could smell it . . .

the garlic, thick aromas of the season's first cutting
mixed among the gas- and body-fumes you shoulder
row by row—if this were what it were . . .
clover, beebalm, the native nouns greening

and growing, work to do. It takes all afternoon.
You'd sleep it off sore and satisfied . . .
onion on your hands, fresh sheets, window flung,
and the fragrance outside turns to fruit—to do again . . .

The Deer

How long did we watch? How long did those
three deer stand pondering the dark, bowing to taste
the least brown grasses, the cold-burnt rosehips,
and whatever else was keeping alive by the creek?
I think of them whenever we lie down this way.
How still they could stand and still tremble.
They leaned to dry earth as to drink.
I think of them when we lie long minutes

through the reaches of winter, not lost ourselves,
nor thirsty, quietly alive in our own dark place.
How our bodies tense to be touched
when we forage in a scatter of blankets.
Once a man laid a deer flat with a single shot.
This gets easier to say. You open both eyes.
You let out your breath and stay still, no matter
how cold the wind, no matter how dark or how near.

The man, who is dead now, couldn't help but smile.
He walked to where the deer fell and knelt as to drink.
I think of them when we lie down this way.
We watched three deer lost under cedars so long
we saw the wind stand still and the tiny ruffle of fur
behind each tense shoulder over each heart was like
our bullet digging in. That's how long. That's how still.
Until our will to love was also our power to kill.

Idyll

I lived behind a window
shaped like a peony
and watched the chickadees
fly into the evening.

I thought they were bats
because they twitched
when they flew too close
to telephone wires

and veered from the crosses
of light thrown
by the far-off city.

I wiped the mullions
with *Fantastik*.
Sat down, got up,
Walked around.

When it began to rain
I called a handy-man
to caulk a hole in the joist.

I wore Oxford button-downs
with thin stipes
and shaved before the sun
was too high.

For a few hours my face
took the light,
and then the chickadees came

and I caught a view
of a flag torn by light,
the saucer lip of a stadium,
and a glass skyline—

then the sky was
the iridescent back
of a Japanese beetle.
The sun thickened

like old varnish
and the reed-slashed meadowlands
rose up, beyond which I could see

to see the chickadees
settling like a rope of smoke
on the other side of the river.

The Back Yard

Out of blueness,
the hummingbird in the privet.
Then silence
shafts the sky.

In it you can hear
a cat yawning,
missiles moving to Griffiss,
a scarf of chartreuse
drying like a caterpillar.

The seeds in the heart
are like plovers lost inland.
Don't try flying with them.
Just feel the lift,
and the horizon

is the color of raspberries
fermenting in the shed.

But then the hummingbird's gone
and the air is a flask
for the henna-tulips . . .

coils of amber
powder down the shaft

as if they've spilled from a white rose
breaking up in the wind.

Then . . .

neither a twig
nor the obelisk of a birch
can measure a distance.

Ocean

Out of her salt hips
poured my umbel.

My mouth full of shells
and her tongue
a lemon bristling my teeth.

Foam flowered
and the black grapes
tasted sweet again.

I smelled fenugreek,
the cherry pit's talcum,
cod drying like a sandy slipper.

An amaryllis of pain
opened in my throat,

and my silence issued
toward the archipelago.

MARVIN BELL

An Old Trembling

Often one wonders what the snake does all day in its pit
to so successfully keep away hands
and be left alone like a solitary zipper
encircling some space from which it has squeezed out all the light
it would seem,
as if no other creature could so love the dark during the day.
And everyone knows about the kiss of the snake.
And everyone knows about the eyes of the snake.
In its mouth is the blue light of old milk.
On its tongue is a map of red rivers.
It knows your body, your own body, like its own.
It begins with your foot, lurking in a boot,
and ends in the venomous sweat of the heart
if you bother it. But whoever leaves alone
whatever in nature wishes not to be disturbed,
he or she will seem like a god,
so unlike a human being,
even to a snake.

Eastern Long Island

Beach grass tangled by wind—the sound rushes
to every nautical degree—
here are torn memories of inlets and canals,
of ponds, bays, creeks, coves, spits and sandbars,
coastal moons and skies, tidal clumps of tiny crabs
that couldn't keep up, seaweed fixed
to stones looking like the heads of Chinese sages,
all criss-crossing the sundial of my dreams.

I dream more when the meteors come—
Earth's face slipping through a comet's tail—
reminder that we steer an unmarked channel,
buoyless, sounding the vacancy of space
where water turns

to take back what it said and deposit on the shore
the exhausted sailor, his tired, complaining boat,
and the wrack of salt water pouring through the slats.

Wasn't anything to be done. Where ships foundered,
where pilgrims settled and pioneers set off,
now contaminant plumes propose
marriage to the aquifer, this being the way it was
when the shark lost teeth to the incoming tide,
and those legs that covet the tide line
were torn from the armored, methodical crab,
and the gull grabbed off the fish closest to the top.

Wasn't anything to be done—not at first
when rapture simmered underwater, and we played
adulthood, taking sea horse and starfish,
nor later when the fishermen
followed their catch to deeper water,
leaving a stain that coated rocks and weeds
and seemed to be of a shade that contained
its own shadow, an undulation in the channel.

Time has not ended. Yet already it is a struggle
to brush away the first few flecks
starlight lent to this crystal's surface, then mute.
Earth's voice, a harmony begun in molten rumble,
rises through surface wash of water and rush of air
to the high pitch of grass blade and ether light.
Those first bits of impurity, that were to ruin
our diamond in the making, at first barely marked it.

I still love the radiance of a dim storm building
where the tide seems to reverse and the sea vibrate,
puzzling perhaps to fresh eyes yet unfazed
by salt wells building under our beds of clay.
At the tide line a fringe of seaweed keeps time,
and wind-whipped sand opaques our cottage windows.
By the boat ramp, disgorged clam shells await
reclamation by the proximate meek, who shall inherit.

Nature

A hand that tries to shake a hand,
an ear pressed against a silver railroad track,
in a place one goes to be alone
called by various names for parts of the body.
Waiting for this, waiting for that.
Swept by the penetrant odor of choked lilies
and the smoke of dark clouds.
Alone by virtue of a garden. And then
with all five senses about to expire,
suddenly a wedding of male and female
in pools of electro-chemical memory
that existed before dawn,
before thick and thin, before the dead thought.
Earth of dusk. Earth of the belly. Earth of the breast.
And heaven the heaven of a slash
that wakes the sea.
All that is better, all that is worse,
whatever is half-formed,
which is to say everything born one of two parents,
every living thing turned round in the cave,
unable to distinguish the unlit road
from the bright slash in the sky,
shall be set free to roam
to find a husband or a wife
with whom to ruminate
on the messages in the footprints of ants and flies
and on the rights of others, too, who live
a few hours only or part of a day
without once hearing a rooster
scare away an angel.

Pulsations

One sees the trees ahead and the shadows underneath them
and feels the heat and humidity. One's foot throbs
like the body of a spider on the concrete sidewalk. One
has a thought or two, then torpor and the ache of fever.
One cannot express it. Yet one can know it completely.

One holds the hand of another in one's own, and sees
a shadow two make together, and sees the darker shadow
ahead, there where it is one is walking to, and the day is hot.
One's head dozes on one's neck even as one walks on.
One's eyes absorb the moist air and do their best to make pictures.

One has a thought about beforehand and another about afterwards.
Then torpor, and the padded planet sticks on its gear. One
goes among the leftover wrappers, the discarded dailies,
the bottle caps and beer tabs and other indications of humanity,
and sees among the litter the constant rearrangement of matter.

One moves oneself a few things about, slowly, surreptitiously.
There was a bird's egg nearly whole on the grass, and one
considered it to be perfectly flawed, its only fall from grace
the skylight through which the baby pecked its way free. One
thought how birds are so little bother considering their numbers.

Further Pulsations

One sees the leaves let go, and sees the leaves falling.
One thinks one sees the future, in the silence, in the interval.
One imagines the leaves releasing well beforehand. One
imagines an umbrella in the rain, the high underside
of a deciduous tree from which the spoiled plenty drops.

One sees that six months of sunlight insist. One sees the flags
raised in protest and salute, and the green pennants flying.
One flies alongside them in one's mind and is happy. One
flies through the air that contains an aura of dry skulls,
the pooled moonlight of memories, the eternity of loss.

In the countryside, one sees the effects of memory.
One views the hallucination of the leaves flying. They
go every-which-way across but only one way in the end.
They flood the air with their tattered bodies, nearly dry,
and plant themselves lightly on the ground in delicate arches.

They carry the true light of autumn in their veins. They
keep their word to time and necessity and never backtrack.
They are composed of everything that ever entered the soil
to which they return when ploughed underfoot or burned.
One smells the leaves burning and thinks of them falling.

STEPHEN BERG

Ritual

We sat on metal card chairs at the edge. Green plastic rugs hid the
    dirt workers flung up when they dug the hole.
A stranger handed me the bronze box, which we passed between
   us, shook,
    held in our laps.
I climbed down, placed it in the hole.
We joked, wept, went home to eat with friends.
Evening snuck in. The spinning earth spun on.
Snow flurries, starlight's unimaginable patterns.

Months later, out of the Little Schuylkill, a trout leaped
as I turned to the purple splash of a flower on the far bank,
jerked my rod, hooked it, played it, lifted it, thrashing, into my
    right hand,
inched over to the bank, smashed its head against a
    rock and,
that night,
saw in the grilled moist meat and fine bones
her wisp of a face.

From "Sabbaths"

VII.

Where the great trees were felled
The thorns and thistles grow
From the unshaded ground,
And so the Fall's renewed
And all the creatures mourn,
Groan and travail in pain
Together until now.
And yet their Maker's here,
Within and over all
Now and forevermore,
Being and yet to be
In columbine, oak tree,
Woodthrush, beetle, and worm,
In song of thrush and stream,
Fact, mystery, and dream:
Spirit in love with form,
And loving to inform
Form formed within itself
As thought, fulfilled in flesh,
And made to live by breath
Breathed into it by love.
The violence past for now,
The felling and the falling
Done, as a mourner walks
Restless from room to room,
I cross the stream to find
On a neglected slope
The woods' floor starred with bloom.

VIII.

What do the tall trees say
To the late havocs in the sky?
They sigh.
The air moves, and they sway.
When the breeze on the hill
Is still, then they stand still.
They wait.
They have no fear. Their fate
Is faith. Birdsong
Is all they've wanted, all along.

MICHAEL BLUMENTHAL

Deep Ecology

for John Mack

My wife stays home and stares at the amaryllis.
She is watching it grow. For hours,
she sits this way, saying, "if you wait
patiently, you can almost see it open."
Tired of talk, the disposable wastes
of intellection, I stay home too,
until, finally, the flower is open,
gazing at us from its mock-bamboo stalk
like a lion's maw. It's bloody gorgeous,
part of the gods' own greenhouse,
right in our kitchen. In a few days,
we'll be going away. "Let's lend it
to our neighbors," says my wife,
who has never read Hegel, "so
its flower won't be wasted."
I turn off the tape, where someone
with a voice harsh as a switchblade
is lecturing on Nuclear Grieving.
I circle my wife's waist and sing.
I am wise once more, like the earth
is wise, and the stars, and a woman
who thinks with her heart, and a man.
And who can afford to preach
who has not known this? And who
can we trust, who would be willing to trade
the deep echo of that flower's bloom
for the empty sound of two hands clapping?

Cherries

Alps de Haûte Provence

After Auschwitz, it's been said, it's no longer possible
to write about cherries. But the cherries were there,
across from the abandoned lavender oil extraction stove,

surrounded by fields of poppy and thistle and lemon balm
in the old, nearly abandoned village of Montmorin,
once controlled by the Moors, and, when we went to pick them,

the air smelled of lavender and rosemary and linden blossom
and thyme, and my son was sleeping against the breast
of my wife, who looked especially beautiful in the late-light

of Alps de Haûte Provence, and the cherries were delicious
against our pallets, turning our tongues a purplish-red,
their juice dripping down our chins, the magpies hovering

over us like priests, the crows pirating the hayfields,
and I found myself with no choice but to bless
the ambiguous God of cherries and magpies and children

and of marriage, to bless the strange God of my eccentric
mother-in-law Yvette, gathering cherries high in the trees,
and to curse the dark God of Auschwitz and Treblinka

and Birkenau and Dachau, relishing the taste of cherries
in my mouth, refusing to believe they are the same God.

The Geologist

Grand Canyon, Arizona, May 1988

He had made a life of stone:
of sandstone and basalt,
of dolomite and shale
and the wild permutations of schist.
Siltstones spoke to him
and the hard crystals of metamorphic rock:
His life became a history
of sediments and erosions,
of deep strata fissured and faulted
into a great transmutation
of flakes and embering chips.
Nights, he spoke in his sleep
of downcutting rivers,
primordial sea floors
crumpled and forced into islands,

only to resubmerge as wandering continents.
He could see the veins of magma
shooting up through the mountain ranges,
he could feel the great unconformities,
the missing pages and sentences
of subsidences and diastems.
All that he loved of the world
was stone and water, water and wind,
Cambrian and Paleozoic. But he was not,
a stupid man, by any stretch
of the imagination. For he never mistook
pyrite for true gold. He was not fool enough
ever to take gneiss for granite.

Meditation on Politics at the Quabbin Reservoir

for Joseph Duffey

All day there has been no peace
from the species that hates its own stillness
so I have come here now,

where the dandelions are mere ghosts
of their former selves, and the reservoir
tongues its way onto the rocks, to find

once more the peace of my own silence,
a small omen of the enduring clarities
that will contain our epitaph (*We saw things*

for what they were, but acted in spite of them).
But now, for a small moment, it is a world
rife with warblers and incipient eagles,

a stillness at midday we can detour
out of the usual urgencies to come upon.
Yet, even here, I have in me a bit

of the non-sequitur: evil thoughts
I cannot disown come upon me, as much mine
as the fine purity I came here in search of.

Sullied thing that I am, I see this day now
for the fine meadow I lie on, and the cruel havoc
that buzzes beneath it. Meadow was never our metaphor,

nor pure light—only the confluence of good and evil
where we meet to become this: possessors
of a merely partial purity, a purely human one.

PHILIP BOOTH

Navigation

Far inland, he
follows the Dipper's
farside pointers
up to Polaris, turns
90° to starboard,
sights down to
Capella, barely
showing above
the low mountains;
his eye, climbing
from there, finds
Cassiopeia, and off
the angled back
of her chair, again
drops to Mirfak,
a dim star in
Perseus, which will,
as the planet re-
volves into dark, give
him his course
to Aldebaran, the
star, if he ever
sails offshore, he
nightly figures
to navigate by.

March Again

Yesterday the tulip shoots, considering.
Today slight snow on the ground, thin snow in the sky.
Through which, barely, the bronze arctic sun.

The pewtery trunks of old Main Street trees.
The four white chimneys next door, the house
where a woman wrote daily; days like today

she couldn't imagine joys out of doors.
Mine are all locked; no key left. I couldn't
go back if I wished. And why should I? Twelve,

still, I'm a good ways out on Tunk Lake,
my handline down a black hole in refrozen ice.
Nobody out there but me. The whole surface

uneven, under an incomprehensible sky.
I'm jigging a bright hook for perch, maybe walleye
or hornpout. For whatever I thought might come.

Seasons

Bear: beware, from the last days
of August far into November. You
too, you Rails, Gallinules, Snipes;

and from brightest October on, you
Scoters, Eiders, and Old Squaws,
stay clear of blinds and gunboats until

new light lifts you into next year.
And you upland targets for gentlemen
who prefer to shoot rather than hunt,

you alder Woodcock, cornstalk Pheasant
and deepwoods Grouse, keep your cover
as maples bear gold and go bare; wait out

the sky until the last Canada Goose
has gone over. You, too, you Deer,
spooked for a moon's month in backlots

and hardwood groves grown thick with
riflemen bright with blaze vests. About jack-
lights and treestands there is, in truth,

no truth you will ever know. But you,
Fox and Bobcat: you loners know your times
to lay low, to leave no sign for dogs,

nor tracks in new snow. As for you Crows,
Skunks, Raccoons, you'll soon feel
in what small regard you're held: mere

target-practice for small-bore men, or
boys not yet within range of Rabbits.
Yet after new Christmas guns, even after

the year turns new, it's you Red Squirrel,
you quick Coyote and Coydog, and you, slow
Porcupine and old Woodchuck, with whom

I most wish to reason with human reason:
as housewives without blaze vests have fatally
learned, hanging out, like you, in their own

backyards, the laws we keep reinventing
aim for what we most value or value least:
on you, on your kind, who have no reason to know,

the law still says there is No Closed Season.

CHRISTOPHER BUCKLEY

Rain/Light

Dimensionless
blotter, daylight
like white ink soaked
away—take the sinking
east and say this
is what it's come to—
cyanic bruise
sutured
at the ocean's edge,
sky thick as your
palm print against
double glazed
window glass . . .

The honey locust
and heavy brambled green
gone grey, slate, stale
as clouds fallen and risen
from the torpor of the lawns.
Gun barrel border
of the seaboard breaking up
for one articulated strand
of sun to rust
along the rose canes
and thinly sound
their thorny stops.

Against the rheumatic
wall you cast
the scenic flourish
of the West—
purple crepe
of the hibiscus flowers,
unwound and wild
on the baranca's ledge, bled
sunward by ground swirls

below the ice plant's
blooms—saffron, rose,
and ice-white—starring
the palisades, like a sky
about to rise
where the calm
pronouncements of air
flourish in the aquatic
limbs of eucalyptus . . .

Sunset filters the air, empty
sound of rain ending
collecting on the ground—
the ghost ship
silhouette of a robin
atop the roof
with a last song
for the coral sea lanes
of the sun . . .

Fifteen billion years,
blue out of
the three-degree dark,
light has misted down
to be here, never
catching up with its own
dispatch and drive.
Each of us,
no more resourceful
than stars, touched
with the abandoned
thought of home . . .

Autumn's End

Nothing takes me back
like the burning leaves,
that summons, incense
and amber cowl, or the must
and fermentation spilling out
from curb-kicked piles

of camphor and chinese elm,
the thorny live oak leaves
taken up across the gravel drives
in a land where gardeners,
in overalls and canvas hats,
(men whose faces are not
so different from those leaves,)
smoke their pipes day long
while smoldering stacks
of sycamore and eucalyptus turn
the blunt corners of the air
and skeins of ash puff
slowly from backyards
and from the gardener's cuffs
as they pause to tap
their pipe bowls out
against the trunks of trees
or the black rubber of their boots—
a land where boxed hedges
of eugenia or bamboo
feather high and seaward,
where smoke amounts
to a recapitulation of the clouds
and reminds you of the last
afternoons for pomegranates
and tangerines, those wind-
fall gifts of oxidized red
and gold proclaiming
that the world is at hand,
yours until the final ghosts
from darkened fires
rise like filaments
on the low blue-grey
edge of light and air,
to shine like music must,
momentarily, to the blind.

Sycamore Canyon Nocturne

But home is the form of the dream, & not the
dream. —Larry Levis

Home again in dreams, I'm walking that foothill road
as the last morning star slips away over canyon walls—
red-gold riprap of creek rock, ferns splayed in the blue
shade of oaks, the high yellow sycamores, oat straw catching
sun at my feet. Wind-switch, then the chalk-thick stillness
saying *angels*, who come down here to dip their wings
and give the water its color.
                                    Yet even when I'm allowed back
along the weedy path of sleep to this green and singing space,
I know someday air will be set between my shoulder blades
and arms and all my bones, and, little more than clouds,
the clouds will be my final lesson until I'm taken off
into some clearer imagining . . .
                                    In exile, it is hard to love God.
What then, must I renounce? The Psalter of evergreens
ringing along Sheffield drive? The loquat and acacia
burning through ocean fog? Can I speak of love
almost a life ago, syllables repeating the skin's sweet salts
and oils like lemon blossoms riding the August heat?

I love the life slowly taken from me, so obviously spun out
flower-like, and for my own use, it seems, against some future
sky—the world, just a small glory of dust above a field
one autumn afternoon—the resinous pines and a back road
full of birds inside you.
                                    What more could wishes be,
who would live there again, sent back among the breathing
acanthus to lift unconsciously with morning and with mist?
I would.
            Moonlight or dreamlight, this is the world, giving
and taking away with the same unseen hand, desires winding
around the soul like fleshy rings on a tree. Where this canyon
levels out, I'd eat the wild sun-red plums, the sweet light
of the juice carrying through me my only hymn.

I know God, old flame wearing through the damp sponge
of the heart, that candle I cannot put out, coming back
each time it seems extinguished. And so I must bless everything,
take anything given me—these words, their polish and pity,

the absence they bear like the winter trees ascending
the ridge, resembling starving angels in the early dusk,
and then the dark, and the broken order of prayer . . .

I know you are listening. Like the sky. And the birds
going over, aren't they always full of light? But to shine
like these trees again, that air hovering on the canyon walls—
sometimes, all I want to be is the dreaming world.

Early Morning—Ucross, Wyoming

The hundred black birds lifting back
into the burning sun, into cottonwoods
and silver poplars, complain a cappella
that someone else is out beneath the sky
to appraise a portion of the green and un-
sung world, wherein some trees list
flower-like toward the bright margin of the east,
where I too find a station in the light,
quiet with my tea—
                so all the birds come
clucking back, two-stepping from their wind-
stuttered flight and bow again to the earth
not far from where a sprinkler registers
its glistening notes across the lawn,
nor far, for that matter, from the first white-
as-paper clouds which assemble orchestrally
above the Big Horn range and mark the muted
distance off.
            But I'm half blind before
these burnished August fields, the haze
riding the flat space out to a vanishing point
in the opened sky, and so turn to foothills
chorused on my left and right, to house shadow
and the blossomed shadows of the plums
which gradually draw back into themselves
with everything they know.
                Yet you begin to feel
this could save your life, this early rising
into a world the calm accompaniments of which
are grass and the sorrowless dispatch of birds,

a world in which you sit still a while
as the tender winds finger waxy willow leaves
or the damasked bells of hollyhocks ascend
their fluted stalks and call to no one, and to you.

You thought you'd had your say about the blue—
oh, the indifference, the emblem of our loss,
or those thin architectures of belief that lead us
nowhere, really, we ever wanted to be.
But here, it's all elemental each azure dawn,
composed and clear, vast and unrehearsed
as each measure of the air we take miraculously
through the wing-beats of our hearts.

TERESA CADER

A Season for Hunting

The hunters are sympathetic,
they do not blame the woman who stepped from her kitchen
into her backyard, white mittens flashing,
or the coastal stormbanks which drenched the leaves
until they shone like masses of small mirrors sewn
onto the branches of sunlit trees,
or the appetite of deer for corn,
the ravage of crops among poor farmers.
Their voice is collective though it comes
from one mouth at a time,
much like the sound of bullets
ricocheting off boulders or zinging through the woods
like a whip, a succession of snapped twigs.
They recite the lessons of high school science,
the fit survive, the weak are eaten.
As for the season, it is marked by orange vests,
carcasses tied to car roofs, posted signs.
Part of the life cycle, they're trying to say,
it's nature we should be afraid of,
that marksman whose shot reaches anywhere.

A Promise

    Plant kernels quickly, three or four together,
as soon as white oak leaves are big as a mouse's ear;
   hill seedlings with soil scooped by hand;
     fertilize with herring which flood
       up stream in heavy rain and spawn.

    To keep dogs from digging up herring, tie
one forepaw to neck for forty days after planting;
   worm and weed and sniff for root rot;
     when stalks reach two feet high,
       plant pumpkin and beans in their shade.

Remember the names you have been given:
succotash, hominy, pone, maize and samp. Pound or boil,
parch in ashes of September fires; fry with hog.
Sweeten nights with distilled mash and grits.
Roast kernels with rind close to embers.

When snows descend, grind and store and hoard;
chop stalks thin for cattle feed; stuff mattresses
with husks, clay jugs with cobs. Dismantle
the goat tusks on your tables and bury them.
A promise to feed is a promise to make hungry.

AMY CLAMPITT

Green

These coastal bogs, before they settle
        down to the annual
business of being green, show an
        ambivalence, an overtone

halfway autumnal, half membranous
        sheen of birth: what is
that cresset shivering all by itself
        above the moss, the fallen duff—

a rowan? What is that gathering blush
        of russet the underbrush
admits to—shadblow, its foliage
        come of ungreen age?

The woods are full of this, the red
        of an anticipated
afterglow that's (as it were) begun
        in gore, green that no more than

briefly intervenes. More brief
        still is the whiff,
the rime, the dulcet powdering, just now,
        of bloom that for a week or two

will turn the sullen boglands airy—
        a look illusory
of orchards, but a reminder also
        and no less of falling snow.

Petals fall, leaves hang on all
        summer; chlorophyll,
growth, industry, are what they hang
        on for. The relinquishing

of doing things, of being occupied
        at all, comes hard:
the drifting, then the lying still.

North Fork

The humped, half-subterranean
    potato barns, the tubers
like grown stones, wet meat
    from underground a bused-in,
moved-on proletariat once
    stooped for, where Paumanok's
outwash plain, debris of glaciers,
    frays to a fishtail,

now give place to grapevines,
    their tendency to ramble
and run on, to run to foliage
    curbed, pruned, trained
into another monoculture—row
    after profitable row
on acre after acre, whole landscapes
    strung like a zither

where juniper and honeysuckle,
    bayberry, Virginia creeper,
goldenrod and poison ivy would
    have rioted, the wetlands
glistening at the margin, the reed-
    bed plumes, the groundsel's
tideline windrows a patina of
    perpetual motion:

here where unrest is everything,
    where driven human
diligence alone could, now or ever,
    undo the uninstructed
thicketing of what keeps happening
    for no human reason,
one comes upon this leeward, mowed
    and tended pocket,

last resting place of slaves, each
    grave marked by a boulder
hardly more than a potato's size,
    unnamed but as dependents of

Seth Tuthill and his wife Maria, who
        chose finally to lie here
        with their sometime chattels,
        and whose memory too is now
            worn down to stone.

Seed

The way it came spinning onto the lawn—
the elm trees' chaffy currency, each piece
with a spot of seed at the center; the katydid-
colored, breeze-littering spindles let fall
by the maples; the squirm of catkins
fattening on the schoolyard poplars;
the way it annually left its smudge
like a bloodletting under the mulberry
in the first weeks of summer:

spring after spring, the same spangling,
smirching rain of it, making way
for yet other excesses—dewed,
swelling, softening to vegetable rot;
the fanged, maculate, pollen-triggering
tigerlily; the bearded rasp and
ripple of the barley; in field after
field, tasseled, seminal, knife-edged,
the green blades' rustle.

Nobody to hear the screams, if there
were any: . . . *found her* (a quasi-
prurient horror as the word went round) *down
in the cornfield. Strangled. And that ain't
all he* . . . Folks those days had trouble
saying it out loud. Some drifter. Never
caught. Whoever first set up the lingam
and called it Shiva—whatever minion of
some gross, overweening stud . . .

But wait. Remember, there was also Krishna,
flute-player, playboy, holding hands with
all the girls: the warm days glistening

with the feckless pollen of him, the nights
alive with yearning, the music of him,
the moist promises. And after? Doing
the reluctant decent thing. In haste,
stood up with by strangers. The neighbors
counting off the months.

Or that other, worse history, unhinted at
so long, appallingly unburdened one night
over a sepia portrait: *The one who died,
the prettiest of them: what really happened—
even in those days, in that family:
you knew!* Or the living issue, the tie
still unacknowledged: *God was cruel*—thus
Mrs. Transome to Denner, servant and
confidant—*when he made us women.*

And Denner: *I shouldn't like to be a man—
to cough so loud, and stand straddling about . . .*
No matter. The moist, channeling silk awaits
the hanging tassel: *And in multiplying I
will multiply thy seed as the stars of heaven,
and as the sand which is upon the sea shore.* Or
as the storm of stuff the cottonwood squanders
in windrows on the sidewalk—even though
for a man to spend it thus

is, it is written, an abomination: as it is for
a woman to abort. See how the last mystery
rises to a travesty. Golf-cart sitcom.
The lingam huge, no joke. Steel-nippled
gorgon madonna of the primal scene.
*I will make a song full of weapons, with
menacing points, and behind the weapons,
countless dissatisfied faces*: thus
turbulent, fleshy, sensual,

eating and drinking and breeding Walt Whitman
(whom Emily Dickinson did not read, having
heard he was a great scoundrel),
celebrating the procreative urge, being himself
without issue: *of wombs and of the father-stuff,
of sexes and lusts, voices veiled* (he wrote),

and I remove the veil—which Edith Wharton
on the dreadful eve (she was twenty-three)
begged to have lifted

("You've looked at statues in museums, haven't you?"
her mother said, and coldly closed the subject):
who, childless, long schooled in discretion,
remembered sitting on the terrace at The Mount
late into the evening, hearing Henry James intone
the *Leaves of Grass*, extolling the father-stuff
above the lake, while fireflies signaled
the unending seedfall, the glinting
feculence of summer.

Shorebirds in Seasonal Plumage Observed through Binoculars

To more than give names
to these random arrivals—
teeterings and dawdlings
of dunlin and turnstone,
blackbellied or golden
plover, all bound for

what may be construed as
a kind of avian Allthing
out on the Thingstead,
the unroofed synagogue
of the tundra—is already
to have begun to go wrong.

What calculus, what
tuning, what unparsed
telemetry within the
retina, what overdrive
of hunger for the nightlong
daylight of the arctic,

are we voyeurs of? Our
bearings gone, we fumble
a welter of appearance,

of seasonal plumages
that go dim in winter:
these bright backs'

tweeded saffron, dark
underparts the relic
of what sibylline
descents, what harrowings?
Idiot savants, we've
brought into focus

such constellations,
such gamuts of
errantry, the very
terms we're condemned
to try to think in
turn into a trespass.

But Adam, drawn toward
that dark underside,
its mesmerizing
circumstantial thumbprint,
would already have
been aware of this.

JUDITH ORTIZ COFER

The Chameleon

I caught a chameleon lizard
in my backyard,
and to please myself
I moved him from a green leaf
to a tree's brown bark,
then to my yellow porch
where he froze in my hand,
his eyes fixed on me
as if waiting for me to change.

But I stayed the same.

I stayed the same,
and kept him behind a screen
until he had given me
all his colors.

Then I opened the door,
but he wouldn't move.
He just kept his eyes on me—
as if waiting for me to change.

Cultivator

Her orchids were meaty, purple organs
she cut from a tree's rotted trunk
at the peak of their bloom. She would skin
a rabbit as if she were carefully
unwrapping a jewel from a velvet case.

The family admired her funereal calm,
the peace that lit her ivory face in grief,
and it seemed that she could slip from her body
like a silk thread easing through the eye
of a needle.

I believed
she was fleshless under those intricate shawls
of black lace—a hollow where a spider
might design a web in the shape of a woman.

My grandmother learned this early:
the voluptuousness of sorrow, how to turn it
into the widow's allure. Her garden
of *flores para los muertos* grew
beautiful, feeding on our misfortunes.

Why There Are No Unicorns

(a fable retold for my daughter)

Because
each species is specialized;
the cow naturally turns to green,
the bird heads for blue.
The unicorn's predilection
was for white—the snowy laps
of virgins. They say
the only way to capture the rare creature
was to lure him with a maiden
wearing wild flowers in her hair,
a flowing gown of blinding white.
In a silent wood she'd pretend
to doze under an oak or sycamore
while waiting for the curly horn
gently to awaken her.
Enticing unicorns soon became
a gentleman's choice
before choosing: required prelude
to the veil and the ring.
Legend has it that nothing
but the subtle scent of untested flesh
would reveal the special beast—no sachets
of heart of mandrake dipped
in freshly slaughtered lamb's blood; nor
bowls of mother's milk sweetened with cinnamon.
But, alas,

it wasn't long before the unicorns became so scarce
that the maiden's test was traded for the dowry.

The moral of the story is: a woman left alone
in a forest with a hope chest waiting at home—
will soon learn to hunt.

MICHAEL COLLIER

Seneca Street

No more the black walnut's delineated
shade and the topped blue spruce
struggling in its overreach. No more
the double-trunked linden, the half-dead
mulberry, the thin maple and gnarled
sickle pear. No more the black cherry
and the weak apple, and, especially, no more
the dogwoods barely visible, fleshed out
now with leaves. And then, no more the two
floors, one of bright oak, the other
of random-width pine—trees all the same.
No more the black, mail-order door locks
that sag on the sagging doors with their
primitive crosses, and no more the anchor
stars that cleave to the brick like barnacles
and their long bolts threading the width
of the house. No more of this precise
nameable world. We will give it up.
We will move to a place vaguely familiar,
larger by rooms, closer to our needs,
which will emerge now as names for a new world.

Consider the Garden

I worry for the broccoli's sake
that it works too hard in this bad weather,
is too anxious to please me, or that it has seen
the eggplant and cucumber expand easily
in lascivious shade and has watched, as I have,
how those vegetables love only themselves,
hoarding their seed until it falls free
of their dark skin.

I want the broccoli to learn the ethic of busywork,
the ramshackle shantytown of green beans,

where piecework is sweet and profitable,
and the tiny delicate blue-and-white flowers
with lavender pistils are like the soft faces
of infants about to be baptized.

Such is my vanity when I look at the garden
that I think I can influence the destiny of plants,
can instruct them, or tell them, with my tending,
about the justice that lies everywhere in the world:
as in the spade I will use this evening
to turn under the row of peas whose leaves burn
with blight, brought on by frequent rain
and evening mist, and the disfigurement
we recognize as judgment in everything.

Landscape

Stupid. But each of us took turns
kicking the barrel cactus, scuffing
the springy, cross-ripped pattern of needles
off the ribbed staves, until it toppled
from its shallow hold on the rocky hill.

Then one of us knelt with the buck knife
and stabbed deep into its side. The blade
coming out clean and flashing in the sun.
The wound healing up with the dark green
of inner rind. Then another one punched

his hiking stick, like a lance, and opened
a seam to make a spigot as rude as a jack-
o-lantern's nose from which the water,
the legendary water would flow.
But even as we smashed it with stones

and finally opened it along its length,
halved almost, and exposed the dense
moist pulp, we felt certain we'd find
the reservoir, the hidden grail of water
that would save us or at least, spilling out

around us and staining the dry earth,
would forgive our fury against the prickly
pear and cholla, our hacking at the barbed
green world, our kicks that sent it all
down hill skidding and tumbling, sparking

the mica hidden in the granite talc.

I Stand beneath the Mountain with an Illiterate Heart

I stand beneath the mountain with an illiterate heart
and grieve the disappearance of frogs.
How many cycles of moonless nights must I endure
before I see the grass anew and hear the song
of its growing, and know, as I did last night
in the early dark, that it is beautiful
for reasons I can't understand.

I stand beneath the mountain with an illiterate heart
and know there is a force beyond imagination
whose mercy is that it shows no mercy
with a blindness proportionate to ours.
Call it the overimagination or flower.
It hovers above the mind with wings, deferential
wings, philosophical wings, nonexistent wings,
and keeps us taut between earth and sky.

I stand beneath the mountain with an illiterate heart
and know that energy formed as a particle somewhere
and grew in size until it reached a critical mass
and blew apart, whereby the idea for order emerged
ironically and grass arrived in box cars on the plains
where it sat for *days* awaiting the open hand
to finish the waters.

I stand beneath the mountain with an illiterate heart
and listen to the sky's pneumonic breathing.
I cannot think and wonder simultaneously.
I cannot use the microscope in *emergency*.
This is proof that days are the enemy of memory.
What I remember lives on paper awaiting fire.
I wrap up stones with pages and place
them in a row that becomes a wall.
I call it poetry and laugh like the river.

I stand beneath the mountain with an illiterate heart
and imagine the clouds as angels.

"This term pain," they say in every weather,
"we do not know. Please explain. Is it like darkness
or water or the face of the deep? Is it like light
or creeping thing? You are all such experts at this charade."

I stand beneath the mountain with an illiterate heart
and watch the frogs disappear. They are being sucked out
through a hole in the sky. I am standing now on the step,
waiting to go. A year is a day. The reel to reel
is wailing. "No," I say. "Yes. I mean no!"

This Is a Blessing, This Is a Curse

No sound from the stone,
which is to say
that I am deaf at last.
I have prayed for this and then
regretted praying.
No voice from the depths
to rise like fish and leap
for my ear.
This is a blessing for my soul
that would not presume.
This is a curse for my heart
that needs to hear.

There Is an Error at the Heart of Desire

Where does she go around the corner?
Is it possible to know before I learn?
What do I see when she is there?
My eyes are useless at the sight of her.

Here I am on the street.
Send me over as a sacred mirror.
I am lost between her shape and form,
a shadow on Church and Pine.

I am a pool outside myself when she is near.
What does she see beneath my surface?
I am ignorant of the *objects* there,
the coins she has wished upon.

My love betrays a hidden stone.
I can not hold her in the rain.
I search for her like a river through hills
but cannot find her for long.

I see her only from a distance
where she is real, absorbed with strange details,
a lion's tooth and spinning wheel.
I guess her name to no avail.

I watch her fade into the air.
She disappears when I most want her.
I wait for her with the patience of water.
She comes to me with a terrible thirst.
I am quenched by the sight of her.
I am renewed by her lips upon my surface.

What can I say to interest her?
My lapping on the shore is not enough.
She is ignorant of those who most desire her.
I am mistaken about her nature.
What remains when she is gone?

How should I think in order to *know* her?
Where does she go beyond her lines?
How does she stay when she is gone?

I have travelled the country
in search of her. The world is a blur
of peaks and valleys. Do I fly or walk?

I am her enemy without knowing,
her ignorant admirer.
I ask the trees to enlighten me.
I wash my eyes with rain.
Why do I think that time should cease
when I behold her?

There is an error at the heart of desire,
the thought of having her,
the thought that water puts out the flame.

I turn away for a while to clear my waters.
What do I see in her absence?
A toothless lion and pile of wool.
A temple floor and scattered straw.

She comes to me in my privation.
She sheds her dress to bathe in private.
It is dark where she swims from spring to spring.
I hold her there in giving arms.
I bend the light of a million stars.

CARL DENNIS

Spring

All the truth you'll ever be able to cull
From the two cardinals perched on a low branch
Of the mountain ash at the end of the yard
Has to be culled now—3:23 P.M., May 23rd—
However unready you are, your habits of attention
Still those of an amateur.

No use running back to the house for the camera.
No use suspending your judgment
Till you feel more confident, till confident friends
Can come over for consultation.
You are the only audience for the one-scene play
Starring the cardinals and the tree
As a horse-tail cloud sails over the chimney.

A gust over Bitner's garage rustles the paper
On the redwood table where you sit wondering
What Mary would feel were she here now.
Nothing wrong with the question
As long as you can answer it by yourself
In this brief conjunction of light and mood.

As blurred as the details are, or as fitful,
Just wait till tomorrow and try to recall their parade
From the paper cups and confetti they leave behind.
The careful entry in your diary will read
Like a weather report in any ship's log:
Wind from the north-northwest at seven knots,
Morning fog and afternoon clearing,
Sunset of blues and violets, starry sky.

Wake up, friend, and look. That noise just now
Was the bang of your neighbor's screen door.
Look how the cardinals keep to their perches
As your neighbor's son and daughter begin to play
In what's left of an afternoon,
Whose passing they'll never be able to prove
As surely as you can if you do it now.

Tune-up

Before tomorrow's timeless beauty of ripples
Scudding in sunlight over Miller's Pond,
An hour today watching the gray-haired mechanic
At Hodge and Elmwood tune my sedan.
It's April 15th and already warm.
As he stands in the bay, listening to the hum,
He wipes his brow on his forearm, hands too greasy,
And I notice the tattoo I've noticed before,
Three roses with the inscription "Manilla, 1950."
No reason to be ashamed that once on shore leave
The young sailor he used to be considered the moment
Worthy of commemoration. Could be he wishes now
He'd had his other good times inscribed indelibly.
Living proof, after he lost his photos and letters,
That his life wasn't empty, that he didn't dream it away
Though the years have stranded him here at Blackwell's garage
In a city he never assumed he'd settle in.
Tomorrow I'll watch the wind send last year's leaves
Scurrying through the woods like birds, and I'll be safe
In the smoky light from the weight of eras.
Today there's time for watching a man gaze off
A moment into the middle distance as if wondering
If he'd squeezed all the joy available from days gone by.
Strange that the past, fixed as it is, is more of a mystery
Than the future, less forthcoming, less predictable.
I know the paths I'll walk tomorrow at the lake
And the hour I'll walk them, rain or shine.
Here on Elmwood the man listening to my car
Can't tell how much of whoever he used to be
Is alive this minute, here or elsewhere,
Both what he managed to do and what he dreamed of doing
As he leaned on a bridge rail and looked down
Long ago at the water rushing around the piers
And heard it churning. Many more overtones then
Than he can hear now in my motor's hum
Which simply tells him this job is finished
And he can turn to another as I drive off
Caught up in the hum arriving from tomorrow.

RITA DOVE

Rusks

This is how it happened.

Spring wore on my nerves—
all that wheezing and dripping
while others in galoshes
reaped compost and seemed
enamored most of the time.

Why should I be select?

I got tired of tearing myself down.
Let someone else have
the throne of blues for a while,
let someone else suffer mosquitoes.
As my mama always said:
half a happiness is better
than none at goddam all.

Dissolve

Dürer rides into the mountains.
It is not madness he is nearing, like Lenz, but madness
he flees: sickness steeped
in religion and a raging fear.

He yearns for sun and parrots.
He hasn't seen the fleas
nesting in rats
unable to find a way over the Alps.

One thousand meters into
the northern slopes,
the spring air
is spiked with iodine.
His eyes clear of film

and breathing is so rich
an experience, he endures it
in gasps. In Venice
he will have figs and dancing lessons—

and promise the mornings to watercolor.

The Great Piece of Turf

(after Albrecht Dürer's Das
Grosse Rasenstück, 1503)

Dug out just before sunrise,
still moist where the roadside dips
into a hollow, each common
closed blossom:

plantain, heath rush,
feathered shoot of yarrow,
creepy Charlie, cock's foot
and a dandelion.

What possessed him
to tote it
home? and why
whenever I see this watercolor—

its charms held lightly
in check, lightly allowed
to carouse—do I see
charcoal bones on a horse

croaking "memento mori"?
*For in truth, art is
implicit in nature, and
whoever can extract it, has it.*

Each blade of meadow
poises discrete
in its moment, abstract.
What road

could I be walking on,
fresh with weeds and
the gnarled insistent
wildflower? Nature holds

a knife to my throat
by the sweaty canal.
I want my piece of earth
on a white cloth,

a block excised
from the living lap
and set before me to mourn:
magnificent edifice

dying before the very eye. . . .

Drizzle

Such a brightness
These two young
Girls give off
As they follow
Their mother
(I guess),
Down rainy Christopher Street,

Singing
The theme
From
The old
Warner Bros.
Cartoons.

It's
Looney!
Whatever
Has
Proceeded

This moment,
Whatever
Has compelled them
To shout

What Porky
Pig
Can only
Stammer.

Who knows
What mischief
Has been
Set in motion?

They chirp:
"That's all,
Folks!"
It's a
Public secret,

And I think
To myself,

It's spring,
Mr. Blues.
You can't fool me
With drizzle.

Nature Poem

Once,
When I lived
In Virginia,

My upstairs neighbor asked
If, at the reading
I was to give

Would any
Of my new poems
Include a bit
Of the surrounding
Landscape,

And I said to her
No, I don't write
About *that*, but,

This was
A false statement.
I could have told her
Behind a certain house
In Illinois,

Is the beginings
Of a prairie.
I loved
The subtle turnings
Of the word
Brown,

I loved
What a
Clumsy movement
Could toss up:
Feathers,
Survival tactics,

Dust
Slanted by
A mid-November's
Light.

And I could have spoken
On behalf of
The New York
Roof gardens in May:
Small tufts
Of Spring,

Near-secret outposts
Tucked within
A city's
Agenda.

I can't tell you why
Certain things make me
Hold my tongue.

I think the conversation
Dwindled
At that point.
Nervous laughter,
Then she walked
Upstairs.

Why wouldn't a poet
Want to broadcast
Such lush noise?
It was spring
In Virginia,
That particular year
A lovely meter.

It was senseless,
And when she missed
The reading,
Didn't I pluck
A stingy blossom?

Too Young to Know

One day, my father chopped down
The old apricot tree
Which used to live in my parents backyard.
My father deflected my anger at him
With a look I heard Muddy Waters sing:
Y'all too young to know.

When I went to my mother
For the truth,
I only heard
What he must have told her:
A vague story about roots
    and basement pipes,
A vague story about branches
    and kitchen windows,
Punctuated by a shrug which meant:
He just does what he does.

The blues don't know nothing about trees
Unless, of course,
It's enlisted the moon
To drag some shadows around,
Unless, of course,
Something jumps up

Out of a hollow log,
A worry you didn't need
To cross your path.

My father's gone,
The tree's a stump,
And I'm still too young to know
If one day, I'll glance
    out my window
At the sycamore,
And cluck my teeth.

JOHN ENGELS

Garden

Who among us can truly say
he outlives the thick matters
of cold? Meantime
the world flowers: foxglove,
hollyhock, calendula wrenched
sunward, cosmos by its own weight,
downsprawled, cumuli
of marigolds, beaded lily stalks,
curl and shrivel of peony leaves,
lightburst of gloriosas,
and from the beds of alyssum, pink
and white, shastas, dahlias,
all grand manner of rose. Thus
summer arrives, bedizened, decorous,
old, male and uncertain, riding
conclusion, unwilling to last.

In March

In March begin to think
of the difficult accumulation of days,
the difficult orders
of their accumulation.

In March reappear
from under the snow the gorgeous
ambiguous trashes of the world,
none of them ever more

than the simple work itself,
but never less. Therefore in March
be especially attentive though
never more than is owing. Be aware

of how the day moves out from itself,
and the white spin of the sun begins its pitch
down to the next day, next and next
of the fiery awakenings, the helpless resurrections.

Meadow

Once in late summer I walked into
the tawny, deer-tramped meadow, found

in a crushed-out hollow
evidence of disport, scatter

of clothing, joyous
stink of the bruised grasses—so turned

in sad confusion back, tried
to disperse myself, but everywhere

along the meanders of the brook
arose the warm reek

of cedars, and the willows
flickered with green light.

Walking to Cootehill

It has been a long walk to Cootehill
and back again, heel and big toe
blistered, the traffic both ways
impetuous along the narrow lanes.
For a mile or more the journey

stank of ditches, at one point
of a sheep's carcass, three weeks
powerfully dead, already on the way
to almost bones. In Cootehill

at Paddy Boyles's Mens' and Boys'
I purchased for its jauntiness
a new cap, grey wool houndstooth foxhunter;
and on the way back,

in one field spotted an old ram
dangling a hoof. Moved on his account,
I shouted to the farmer, who,
beating dust from his cap against his leg
and wiring shut the gate,
threw over his shoulder *tis only*

a torn, no moren a fookin torn!
making it clear
he believed I had reproved him,
and coming back a little way

let me know I was less by far
than halfway from Cootehill, hinting

I was maybe even losing ground.
Behind me, the lane narrowed
onto distances from which diminished
the monotonous, pained bleatings
of the ram. Whitethorn and wild roses

were in raucous bloom. From everywhere
in the hedges came great chirrupings
and bustle of chaffinches,
cattle lowed, the sky
sputtered with light. I limped
along the dwindling lane, wary
of cars, suspicious
of the ditches out of which
some skittish creature, the instant
I least expected it, likely
would flush—as on my way

doves had erupted in wild flight,
hares skidded
on the macadam, and from deep
in the roadside skullcap had come
little angular breakneck skitterings. Now,

at last safely back, and wearing
this new cap, I posture where
my images converge between
the four mirrors of the Music Room,
before and behind and to either hand
grinning and scowling, cocking
the cap over one eye, then the other, alert
for the least anterior glint
of bald spot—in fact, I look,

wearing this cap, my age,
and consider returning it; in fact
I so greatly fail to be pleased
that it rockets up on garish exhausts

of question marks, exclamation points,
asterisks, arrows, stars,
to shudder, hover and bare
to the general mockery
my unbecoming skull.

—Annaghmakerrig, August 1990

Landslide

    By first light the pines struck down into the meadow.
Only an hour before the clouds had been heavy, shadows
        buried the rafters, and light scurried
    window to window. But then

        the snow began to flicker, clouds to deform,
    and from the incandescent line of the peak
proceeded a ragged scrolling of light, finally
    the sun itself clearing the highest ridge,
        bearing with it a wind so violent
    that nothing in the stunned world knew more
        than that something must have changed. At 5 a.m.,

    the house cold, cold light billowing and the hibiscus
        abloom in the north window, dark clouds low,
        gold-bellied over the snowy yard, the sky

paling and bold against it two engorged blossoms
                         backlit by snowshine, star-hearted purple-to-
vermilion
            where the petals overlapped, I looked up at the mountain
and from just beneath the shoulder of one shimmering ridge

            occurred an abrupt enlargement of shadow
                      from out of which the mountain stormed,
                         bearing before it colossal froth of mud, boulders, trees,
               bright explosions of brooks and ponds, snow clouds, all

soundless, therefore suggesting nothing of danger
            so that I felt no need to run
                         before the landslide until at last
            it cascaded over the head wall into the valley
and crested in a roar of dust and snow
at the road's crown and overran the house
where I had been standing at the porch window brave
            with amazement. Too late

I discovered myself to have failed
            to escape, to have been borne down
                      by house and mountain, my cheek
                            crushed into a sour
                                  linoleum, my breath
                  irretrievable, on my eyelids ant,
earwig, spider, the house above me still
            and orderly in ruin that theretofore most ordinary
                      of all mornings when merely to have looked
up at the mountain from the swollen buds
and blooms of the hibiscus, of all things red
            most red, had been enough

                               to commence the overbalancing
                  into that swirl, billow, upheaving dome
            of ice and shadow where I was about to die,
                  or was already dead, or must describe
            which it was to be.

—for Don Sheehan, at The Frost Place, August
1988

CAROL FROST

Refusal

Violently, because the acres were not smoothed with topsoil, she
     wrenches
the handmower into places the rider won't reach. Afraid of snakes.
     Hating the thistle.
A keening from blade hitting rock goes into her ear like an insistent
     beak in alder,
     and she stops, repulls the starter, and leans in hard again to move
     the engine
through the undergrowth. Her tall boys, men really, and their father
     have long since
ceased wanting to know why, sweating, thorn-tattooed, she pushes the
     doubtful edges
     of the yard back, cutting paths through a dead predecessor's orchard:
not to name wildflowers or to watch the delicate metamorphoses
     unfold & unfold
in green billowed darkness; not to smell mint. How to describe the
     beauties of this
violence and this fatigue, even to herself? Isn't there a human stillness
     in shapes labored
     over, and comfort to be taken from feeling nature's refusal to be
     much moved?

Being

Being a deer means grazing, suddenly lifting the head
     and turning it straight into your own: tomorrow,
this evening, in a field of autumn browns where you walk. Absorbed in
     its dangers—
having you always at its neck as it eats and breeds and goes past—
     you feel its stillness lodge deep inside you,
and you stay there, wrapped into yourself, as things drift. To be
     completely deer
means outlasting twilight in a field which you begin to think was
     barely there before

the deer stepped from the forest edge, setting forth just a little of itself,
    just the head and shoulders,
without sound, until, suddenly, it snorts and spills itself—
    having sensed you, over the scent of grasses, who were invisible.

Sexual Jealousy

Think of the queen mole who is unequivocal,
    exuding a scent to keep the other females neuter
and bringing forth the colony's only babies, hairless and pink in
    the dark
of her tunneled chamber. She may chew a pale something, a root,
find it tasteless, drop it for the dreary others to take away, then demand
    more; she must suckle the young. Of course
they all hate her and are jealous of the attention given her
by her six bedmates. In their mutual dream she is dead and her urine
    no longer arrests their maturing. As irises infallibly unfold,
one of their own will feel her sex grow quickest and greatest. As
    they dig
together, their snouts full of soil, they hope this and are ruthless in
    their waiting.

Papilio

Collecting is a basic human trait. The great collectors
found the Nabokov Pug, *suvarovius* flying by the hundreds,
and the common glider, then spread their wings, medicating them
so carefully that no corruption invaded; they placed
them in beautifully carved bureaus to remember
the graceful madnesses of their flight over the white clearings,
the dark green ferns, the wildflowers, and the peculiar, crooked
    branches
of the thornapple like crucifixions. Some lay their eggs near violets;
some need the salts and minerals in animal urine;
most are diurnal. The only time I held one in my hand
was when I found it in my garden, fanning itself
on a bean plant. It seemed to have muscles in its wings,
but all I could see, on closer inspection, were its veins, its curled
    proboscis,

and its horrible compound eyes, like those on the fallen preening
    angels
of the imagination. I like to think that its letting me pick it up
was sign of its complicated instinct for survival—in the way its
    eyespots
can persuade birds to peck at a dispensable part of its wings.
When I let it go, it wafted over to the barn wall.
What trick of pen or brush could capture that slightness
of flying? No wonder they are pinned to boards, romantics exaggerate
their delicacy, and modern poets dislike them. But they are not frail.
Think of their long thin hearts pumping yellow blood, their concealed
    poisons,
and their pheromones and colors which are sexual—they grow
    transparent
from sex. They are also territorial. Think of the rate of speed of
    autumn.

ALICE FULTON

A Little Heart to Heart with the Horizon

Go figure—it's a knitting performance every day,
keeping body and clouds together,
the sky grounded. Simulcast, ecumenical
as everywhere, stay and hedge
against the bet of bouffant space,
you're the binding
commitment so worlds won't split.

Last week we had Thanksgiving.
The post–cold warriors held a summit
full of East meets West
high hopes. Why not hold a horizon?
Something on the level, equitable instead.
They said the U.S. Army held rehearsals
on monastic sand. In the desert,
lieutenants zipped in camouflage
thought back to where horizons were
an unmade bed, a nap
on the world's edge. Privates, nights
when they were sanded
by flower fitted sheets, ground out
in flower fitted skin: her, oh him.

This Michigan is short on mountains,
long on derricks
needlenosing heaven, making evil
electromagnetic fields.
"Talks on the fringes of
the summit could eclipse
the summit itself," the anchor
admitted. Go figure.

Your reticence, your serene
lowness, because of you I have something
in common with something.
Your beauty is *do unto me* and who am I

to put you in the active voice?
I rest my case
in your repose, a balance
beam, point
blank closure
that won't—bows are too ceremonious—

close. You graduate
in lilac noise. You take off
and you last.
You draw all conclusions
and—erasure, auroral—you
come back. But I am here to vanish
after messing up the emptiness.
I am here to stand
for thanks: how it is
given, hope: how it is
raised. I am here to figure
long division—love—
how it is made.

A.M.: *The Hopeful Monster*

So dawn. A morcellation of the dark, the one
dumb immaculate gives way.
Appetite and breakfast.
          The light is enlarged
to show detail. It strokes the earth
with no boring or fumbling, with just
          enough. So dawn. Like charity it spreads
itself thin, "envieth not, vaunteth not,
beareth all things . . ."
It circulates
but has no currency;
          it scraps the dark
for fluctuation and rough justice,
puts a lean on the fields,
glittering like insect flesh.
          A vastation, it braces
every thistle, scrub, and burr. Each minnow, morsel,

swimming in its limber glue, each cell
      strung with elation. The dirt dances in yields.
Look at it that way and give
wonder. The light is enlarged to show detail.
      It bareth all things, it maketh all things
naked, a slater, stripping
the flesh from the hide.
It circulates, but has no currency.
      It takes shape from what blocks it,
the obstacles, like criticism, a kind of birth
control. So scathe
the one who made the pus and suffering
of the stray. He has twenty-six toes
and twenty-six claws to break the spines of mice.
Fleas suck his blood
      and that's how he will die. Nice nature,
nice. Kitten is a pretty thing,
bred to pet. "Cute" is a baby
human concept. Toddler in utopia,
      undergulfed by nothing all
the night, give wonder. And give fear.
Everything that knows it lives
is shivering. Everything
that lives predicts.
      Terror is just
the confidence of prophecy:
what from the gut
the nerve emerges—
      step by step and sweat by sweat.

Becoming a Redwood

Stand in a field long enough, and the sounds
start up again. The crickets, the invisible
toad who claims that change is possible,

And all the other life too small to name.
First one, then another, until innumerable
they merge into the single voice of a summer hill.

Yes, it's hard to stand still, hour after hour,
fixed as a fencepost, hearing the steers
snort in the dark pasture, smelling the manure.

And paralyzed by the mystery of how a stone
can bear to be a stone, the pain
the grass endures breaking through the earth's crust.

Unimaginable the redwoods on the far hill,
rooted for centuries, the living wood grown tall
and thickened with a hundred thousand days of light.

The old windmill creaks in perfect time
to the wind shaking the miles of pasture grass,
and the last farmhouse light goes off.

Something moves nearby. Coyotes hunt
these hills and packs of feral dogs.
But standing here at night accepts all that.

You are your own pale shadow in the quarter moon,
moving more slowly than the crippled stars,
part of the moonlight as the moonlight falls,

Part of the grass that answers the wind,
part of the midnight's watchfulness that knows
there is no silence but when danger comes.

Rough Country

Give me a landscape made of obstacles,
of steep hills and jutting glacial rock,
where the low-running streams are quick to flood
the grassy fields and bottomlands.
                                        A place
no engineers can master—where the roads
must twist like tendrils up the mountainside
on narrow cliffs where boulders block the way.

Where tall black trunks of lightning-scalded pine
push through the tangled woods to make a roost
for hawks and swarming crows.
                                        And sharp inclines
where twisting through the thorn-thick underbrush,
scratched and exhausted, one turns suddenly

to find an unexpected waterfall,
not half a mile from the nearest road,
a spot so hard to reach that no one comes—

a hiding place, a shrine for dragonflies
and nesting jays, a sign that there is still
one piece of property that won't be owned.

Lion of God in Vermont in May

—for Maurice

The black flies have not yet arrived, and our dog
is merry. Three-petal chords of trillium go singing
past fiddleheads, trippling over ladyslippers and bone-
pale skeletal leaf-lace, ghosts of a spent fall's meaning-
ful maple blood sugar sipped back to root. Dandelions
spark meanwhile up in shades still April-thin, charge

star-yellow with seedy largesse. To swell the charge
the plucked eye scatters. Bless the tooth of the dog
and cynic angel, electric cloud and tongue of lion;
invisible, visible, in between . . . all singing
throughout. Gnats', neutrinos', glaciers' meanings
pollen May's counterparts, seen and unseen. Such bone-

close tremulo begs for Norse Epic's lyric bone,
a funny elbow to nudge with, a wink to discharge
excess, ecstatic froth. May no demeaning
oath rule out bow-wow or hot saliva. Our dog
likes his Pastorals spiked with unseemly singing
and scenes to make chaste scenery blush; and lions

in burly prides agallop. Or if not lions
on the lam, Vermont's own coyotes, all prance-prime bones
fleshed for chase, whiffly bloodspice, swift shapes singing
with moon-bravado back to him. Ariel. His dreams charge
aerobic through lyric pansy beds, his dogged
sleep sights turning a velvet faces growl-worthy, meaning

his toes twitch, his nose flares in pursuit of wild meanings
run down and caught fast as his sleep. A sunflower lion
was plenty excuse once, for Ariel—brave puppydog—
to stack and pose for. Shore-gallant he hoards the beached bone
that made him (once briefly) Amagansett King, nobly charged
with fetch and deposition, with showery singing

wet blessings. As Cerberus he heels to a singing
ferryman, worried his Styx over waves of meanings
three noses could not fathom. As for lions
in these Green Mountain pastures, Ariel has been charged,
by black flies not so far off, to lie like a good dog
(to himself) in wait. He nibbles an endless MilkBone,

Our Ariel, content to plot with singing lions and dream
the charged geometry of May, is dazed with meaning
moreover, boning up on the being of immortal DOG.

Curious Experiments

1. "Schrodinger's Cat"

I don't think it's been done, but it's been said
to illustrate Schrodinger's quantum wave
theory better than most hard lab-work would:

> You put a cat in a box, one that you have
> rigged up with a capsule of poison gas that will,
> on being released, kill instantly. The trigger's
> a single atom's decay—a random control,
>
> not yours—as to the moment—but dead sure,
> inside the given space of time the cat
> must serve, with no parole, to fire. The death,
> enclosed, is silent; you, meanwhile, must wait—
>
> however curious (don't hold your breath)
> you are, however eager to end the game
> by opening the box ahead of schedule.
>
> The cat is not made conscious of this; the same
> cannot be said of you, in waiting, the real
> and only subject of this maddening trial.

The point in question is light (I mean, not grave).
It's this: to ask yourself if the cat is dead
at any moment of your watch, or alive.
The answer: both; in limbo, equally evil/good.

2. The Galactic Axion Experiment: Looking for "Wimps"

Some physicists guess that most of all matters we know
(the universe, that is) is made of what we do
not know, particulate "dark matter" known to flow
(invisibly as blessings) "out there" and inside us, too.

They're searching for the so-called "axion"—impossible
to see, feel, touch, or make any image of—
ubiquitous, and strictly hypothetical,
a sort of "Weakly Interacting Massive

Particle" (WIMP for short). Such would make up
all but a single cent of the universe
thus permeated, with no known effect or scope.
How horrible, how dark, and how perverse!

The doctorals pray this matter, in proper measures
recorded in copper, will resonate—though ever
so faintly—unheard by us, but as music to God's ears.

3. Playing against Time

This dot will come, to be filled, to breathe and cry
her liquid salty amniotic air
and practice, in the dark, a given score

with almost sinister dexterity.
She sight-reads by touch, as if her budding body
and wit had seen through years of scales, as if

she'd got the patterns by heart alone—whole, half
steps, accidentals fixed to code each key
for one, no random, base, a note called "home."

The point is to get all there, in her nearly sound-
proof chamber, technique fine-tuned for the concert hall.
Her heart's set on beating a deadline no metronome

prepares one to meet. Suddenly pushed from behind,
her mother in the wings, it's time . . . ? Time alone won't tell.

4. Pandora's Frame of Mind

My child, no more than a thought-experiment
performed, as on Schrodinger's cat, in the dark
as to any one blessed moment, seems heir to the event
of one electron bursting a core, that weak click

of random energy, its decay. Yet, one still loves
considering this state of things, where not
a single one of the particular bodies that
concatenate a cell, as it lives and moves

toward consumation, reveals intent or minds
the state the whole is in. Each molecule,
enchained by chance and rote, itself an all
and nothing realm, counts nothing out of bounds
save prying its closed case open, as Pandora did
to her curiosity's credit, as Zeus' dot intended.

Hers too was just . . . a question, borrowed, of time
spent picturing possible contents, frame by frame . . .
a stop-gap, the reel run through . . . then open . . . ended.

5. This Canned Galactic Music, Again

Magnetic coils, liquid helium, a copper pipe,
not tuned to the human ear, but to the perfect pitch
of microwaves, atomic shells, what is picked up,
if at all, by rods of synthetic sapphire, each
a single crystal: such is the "wimp detector."

The hope: to ruffle alien music out of the dark,
hook it on crystal frequencies, as by clockwork
the rod sweeps through the soup, its sapphire register.

Perhaps God is not dead, but alive in wimps.
The trick is to tune in on what wimps answer to
in material terms. So far, what has turned up,
re: "galactic axions," puts no Copernican crimps
in matter's be-all and end-all, such as we hope

to be and end it. As for seeing through a wimp's
design or, for that matter, God's: must we take no view?

DONALD HALL

Surface

The surveyor climbs a stonewall into woods
scribbled with ferns, saplings, and dead oaktrees

where weltering lines trope themselves into stacks
of vegetation. He sees an ash forced around a rock

with roots that clutch on granite like a fist
grasping a paperweight. He stares at hemlocks

rising among three-hundred-year-old sugarmaples
that hoist a green archive of crowns: kingdom

of fecund death and pitiless survival. He observes
how birch knocked down by wind and popple chewed

by beaver twist over and under each other, branches
abrasive when new-fallen, turning mossy and damp

as they erase themselves into humus, becoming
polyseeded earth that loosens with lively pokeholes

of creatures that watch him back: possum, otter,
fox. Here the surveyor tries making his mark:

He slashes a young oak; he constructs a stone
cairn at a conceptual right-angle; he stamps

his name and the day's date onto metal tacked
to a stake. His text established, he departs

the life-and-death woods, where cellular life keeps
pressing upward from underground offices to read

sun and study slogans of dirt: "Never consider
a surface except as the extension of a volume."

Pluvia

In the nation of rainy days
    tractor-trailers spray and glissade
gray through rain down blacktop
    with a sound like cloth tearing;
an airplane circles above clouds
    that conceal the balding mountain
and engine-sounds waver like a dream
    voice saying, "please, please,"

In the nation of rainy days,
    the white cottage downstreet vanishes
into gray air, disappearing
    like a vessel lost in a hurricane;
rain draws wavery vertical lines
    against the black doors of a barn
and chimneysmoke kneels on flattened
    grass, praying to dissipate.

In the nation of rainy days,
    clouds hang tatters of shaggy muslin
as pale as winter on maples
    that sink like shipwrecked cottages;
deer lost in overgrown orchards
    dissolve in the mist and drizzle;
abandoned by honeybees, old roses
    and soaked clover curve earthward.

Day after day, we wake to green rain
    drenching the garden; we slog
through our chores slow-dancing
    to rain's brute tune that drones
the same saturated phrase in the same
    cadence again and again
like a lost airplane still circling
    over the nation of rainy days.

"Winter's asperity mollifies . . ."

Winter's asperity mollifies under the assault of April.
   Now the trout fisherman flexes stiff waders;
now cattle and sheep clamber out of barns that kept them warm all
  winter;
    now the countryman no longer seeks comfort

by sleeping on his Glenwood, for ice has departed the coldest field.
   Under the new moon animal bodies play,
cavorting on tender grasses that the breezes caress and embrace.
   Each morning we gaze at daffodils, closing

our eyes in languor. Soon we will inspire the July garden's densest
   effluence and shuffle to drowse in maple
shade and the shade of birches, convening where soft mosses are
  softest
    to build with our bodies temples for Venus

as summer suggests: We sigh, we are easy—because we understand
   that we must squeeze every moment: The truest
aphrodisiac is our certain knowledge that we will die: We sweat,
   we pant, we drop our pants whenever we touch

the subject of dying—because dead people rarely appear content;
   because they want energy; because they lack
desire for each other's bodies. In response to death's deplorable
   likelihood, we bed each other down in spring.

"Mount Kearsarge shines . . ."

Mount Kearsarge shines with ice; from hemlock branches
snow slides onto snow; no stream, creek, or river
   budges but remains still. Tonight
    we carry armloads of logs

from woodshed to Glenwood and build up the fire
that keeps the coldest night outside our windows.
   Sit by the woodstove, Camilla,
    while I bring glasses of white,

and we'll talk, passing the time, about weather
without pretending that we can alter it:
       Storms stop when they stop, no sooner,
            leaving the birches glossy

with ice and bent glittering to rimy ground.
We'll avoid the programmed weatherman grinning
       from the box, cheerful with tempest,
          and take the day as it comes,

one day at a time, the way everyone says.
These hours are the best because we hold them close
       in our uxorious nation.
          Soon we'll walk—when days turn fair

and frost stays off—over old roads listening
for peepers as spring comes on, never to miss
       the day's offering of pleasure
          for the government of two.

DANIEL HALPERN

The Approach

Let what declines find a level of its own.
The early evening's shorter,
the afternoon not much more

than a little late sun
coming in over whatever landscape
you might have found to rent or purchase.

But that part of the night
into which you wake with thoughts
of last waking

lasts a childhood year.
The birds of the pre-dawn,
loosely present symbols

of suspension, the hovering spirit
renaissance helium, finally rising
beyond the edge with a vengeance,

as Piero's defiant Christ-in-fresco lifts
over his sleeping guards
who abandon their duty to this world

and the sprawling medieval landscape
in Borgo San Sepulcro—the rocks of exit
nowhere in sight,

but his leg cocked on the wall
as he sees again
although for the first time

the surviving air of his last leaving.
It is with something like satisfaction
that we undo the handiwork of the unimaginable,

give back the disharmonious
theories of season, its rising
and falling, the guards at last coming around.

Annuals

The trees hold against
their stark red anger—
the falling off of
another season,
another shedding
of the carapace
soul to stand open
before ungracious
seasonal winds.

We've been fired-up,
we've been ecstatic
in the hungry warmth—
endless August days
at summer's cool end,
too bright for deep thought,
too cheerful, so full
of the promised light
illuminating
what-comes-next. Today
the woods are ever-
green, with both winter-
stripped trees and those spared
alight in the fields,
drab green fired-up,
this empire's time
running out, color
the correct landscape
to show what's left you.

Wolf Warrior

(for all the warriors)

A white butterfly speckled with pollen joined me in my prayers yesterday as I thought of you in Washington. I didn't want the pain of repeated history to break your back. In my blanket of hope I walked with you, wolf warrior, and the council of tribes to what used to be the Department of War to discuss justice. When a people institute a bureaucratic department to serve justice then be suspicious. False justice is not justified by massive structure, just as the sacred is not confineable to buildings constructed for the purpose of worship.

I pray these words don't obstruct the meaning I am searching to give you, a gift like love so you can approach that strange mind without going insane. So we can all walk with you, sober, our children empowered with the clothes of memory in which they are never hungry for love, or justice.

An old Cherokee who prizes wisdom above the decisions rendered by departments of justice in this world told me this story. It isn't Cherokee but a gift given to him from the people in the North. I know I carried this story for a reason and now I understand I am to give it to you. A young man, about your age or mine went camping with his dogs. It was just a few years ago, not long after the eruption of Mount St. Helens, when white ash covered the northern cities, an event predicting a turning of the worlds. I imagine October and bears fat with berries of the brilliant harvest, before the freezing breath of the north settles in and the moon is easier to reach by flight without planes. His journey was a journey towards the unknowable, and that night as he built a fire out of twigs and broken boughs he remembered the thousand white butterflies climbing toward the sun when he had camped there last summer.

Dogs were his beloved companions in the land that had chosen him through the door of his mother. His mother continued to teach him well and it was she who had reminded him that the sound of pumping oil wells might kill him, turn him towards money. So he and his dogs traveled out into the land that remembered everything, including butterflies, and the stories that were told when light flickered from grease.

That night as he boiled water for coffee and peeled potatoes he saw a wolf walking toward camp on her hind legs. It had been generations since wolves had visited his people. The dogs were awed to see their ancient relatives and moved over to make room for them at the fire. The lead wolf motioned for her companions to come with her and they approached humbly, welcomed by the young man who had heard of such goings on but the people had not been so blessed since the church had fought for their souls. He did not quite know the protocol, but knew the wolves as relatives and offered them coffee, store meat and fried potatoes, which they relished in silence. He stoked the fire and sat quiet with them as the moon in the form of a knife for scaling fish came up and a light wind ruffled the flame.

The soundlessness in which they communed is what I imagined when I talked with the sun yesterday. It is the current in the river of your spinal cord that carries memory from sacred places, the sound of a thousand butterflies taking flight in windlessness.

He knew this meeting was unusual and she concurred, then told the story of how the world as they knew it had changed and could no longer support the sacred purpose of life. Food was scarce, pups were being born deformed, and their migrations, which were in essence a ceremony for renewal, were restricted by fences. The world as all life on earth knew it would end and there was still time in the circle of hope to turn back the destruction.

That's why they had waited for him, called him here from the town a day away over the rolling hills, from his job constructing offices for the immigrants. They shared a smoke and he took the story into his blood, his bones while the stars nodded their heads, while the dogs murmured their agreement. "We can't stay long," the wolf said. "We have others with whom to speak and we haven't much time." He packed the wolf people some food to take with them, some tobacco, and they prayed together for safety on this journey. As they left the first flakes of winter began falling and covered their tracks. It was as if they had never been there.

But the story burned in the heart of this human from the north and he told it to everyone who would listen, including my elder friend who told it to me one day while we ate biscuits and eggs in Arizona. The story now belongs to you too, and much as pollen on the legs of a butterfly is nourishment carried by the butterfly from one flower to another, this is an ongoing prayer for strength for us all.

After All

After all   the hard noise
the wind toss   in fragrance

even her footsteps
sway, displease   her tranquil arms
                   and a fern, bends

every instant   through my tired body
we tremble   together in white

We Are Made

We are made   pure by power
so pure like stone   upon stone and water

oceans bruise my hand
for the salt they carry   soft and in love
                  moves deeper to the green

I lift my hands   maker of fists, honorary
all that is left simple   runs down my veins.

House Is Empty Now

House is empty now   with my hand
upon skull and mantle   the letters tumble

a crevice, alone. Seek
coming, never receiving   the elixirs, up in the sky
                  catch them, a spark

never closing.   Who is there, now?
A teaspoon, yellow   flower-mirror.

A Crack inside My Breast

A crack inside my breast
clap and a tiny tree falls

split through bone
a knot tightens

in my throat. It is not a knot
especially the right one

flickers, no more my eyes
the knot pushes down

a needle rises, every circle
this is how I write

I walk out in the open, so
juices, nerves and stones.

WILLIAM HEYEN

Grace

Hundreds of thousands dead this week in Bangladesh.
Within this Brockport acre, spring's first warblers
whistling in tangles of wild grapevine & red osier.

Photos of swollen bodies of humans & farm animals
eddying in receding waters, & desperate sticks begging.
Along my street, plum & apple ornamentals in thick bloom.

Mother Teresa, the living saint, appears with food
& clothes & her consoling arthritic hands
above the infected flood. What world is this, then,

Lord, where your crazy grace, it seems, is levelled
without regard for virtue or sin, & someone still
believes in you with the deepest blossom

of her heart? And *acts*? From the beginning,
You've not planted enough trees in Yourself, have You,
& are not become, are You, the rapture we pray for—

but the holy woman asks me in my lucky comfort
not to curse for her, & her wrists are parchment
on which is written the answer to my question.

Fur

Reports of a lone lynx in village yards.
Searching for another of its kind,
it has trespassed from the Adirondacks,
but will not find another here.

We seem to glimpse it between buildings & cars,
its tufted ears, tawny shape, black-tipped
short tail, but it's just business & traffic,
as usual. Even our trees are tame.

We want something, but don't know what.
Evenings, we appear in relief,
kids & chlorine on our minds,
but still yearning & on the prowl. . . .

We have come to this loneliness one
killing at a time. Our eyes gleam
out of the dark mindless mowing of our lawns,
& TV. Look at us. Look at me.

Canary

When, to check, I swung my headlamp from the coal,
my canary had collapsed. I grabbed its cage
& got the hell out. Well,
that was the old days, before electric sensors, my wage
barely a living, & black lung, by forty. My wage
barely a living, & black lung, by forty.

For now, at twentieth century's end, I live longer
& send my kids to college. They study
making money, or how frogs die out over
the whole world. In poetry,
a frog is a canary. In poetry,
a frog is a canary.

I've learned, during my own lifetime or so,
by way of webbed foot & wing & long sticky tongue,
to croak & sing: gray snow
feathers the coal frogs forming here & there
& everywhere, forever. Here & there
& everywhere, forever.

Wish

In my dream, my car is an aquarium.
I'm on the hood, prone, looking in,
wondering how I could ever drive again.

It's evening, my interior lit with tropical fish
& desire for a new life. I didn't know
I was this tired. I place my forehead

against the windshield, close my eyes, & wish
for you know what. In the beginning, friend,
every word was a dreaming plant or animal

until our traffic changed everything, but something
seems to be happening for the better, now,
if only it's not too late. I fall asleep

against this glass until I wake, a few
guppies & angels convulsing in the drying soul
of the world until our ecstasy, &/or our end.

EDWARD HIRSCH

Summer Surprised Us

These first days of summer are like the pail
of blueberries that we poured out together
into the iron sink in the basement—

a brightness unleashed and spilling over
with tiny bell-shaped flowers, the windows
opened and the shrubs overwhelming the house

like the memory of a forgotten country, Nature,
with its wandering migrations and changing borders,
its thickets, woodlands, bee-humming meadows . . .

These widening turquoise days in mid-June
remind me of slow drives through the country
with my parents, the roads spreading out

before us like the inexhaustible hours
of childhood itself, like the wildflowers
and fruit stands blooming along the highway,

the heat tingling on my skin that would
burn with the banked fires of adolescence
and the no less poignant ache of adulthood

on those long detours through the park
during the last rain-soaked nights of spring
and the first beach-days of the season . . .

It's the leisurely amplitude of feeling
that rises out of these expanding afternoons,
the days facing outward, the city taking notice

of itself after all these months, off-duty,
wearing short sleeve shirts and sleeveless dresses
the color of sunlight, the texture of morning.

It's the way we move toward each other
at night, tired, giddy after a day together
or a day apart, flush with newborn plans

for a holiday from daily life, in reality.
We are festive and free-floating. We are
poured out like a bucket of wild berries.

In the Midwest

He saw the iron wings of daybreak struggling
to rise over the warehouses stacked along the river.

Rotting wharves and bulkheads. Dead tracks
leading to railroad yards on the edge of nowhere,

the sun toiling in gray smoke on the horizon.
As if God had crumbled bits of charcoal

in the air and dusted the earth with ashes—
Eyelids of silt, thou shalt not open!

Scourge of asphalt and carbon, of slag heaps
and oil-stained piers, of soot and smog . . .

He was not a real prophet, I suppose,
not the biblical kind, like Habakkuk or Amos,

and yet he wandered through the heartland alone
and saw the shattered spine of a bridge

collapsing in Gary; he saw the ruined breath
and gaping windows of a factory choking

in Youngstown; he saw the stench of history
seeping out of Sandusky and Calumet City . . .

Stops on the highway, stains on a dark map.
Foundries, industrial waste. Stripped quarries,

stripped land, what we've done to the sky
curdling over two drunks sleeping on an embankment

and waking up to a late day in the empire.
He kept speaking of Byzantium, of Constantinople.

He saw gulls feasting on garbage.
He saw the gouged bodies of the unborn.

First Snowfall: Intimations

How long it has taken me to recall
That cold and radiant afternoon
                           in late October, 1959,
When twenty-five squirming bundles
Of trouble were subdued
                     and then transfixed
By a bright snowfall that drifted
                        and gusted like leaves
Outside the prison-like windows of Peterson School.

To us, it seemed as if someone
Was dusting off the rooftops
                     and high ceilings of winter,
Dropping sheets of paper, wet and unlined,
From a cloudy, invisible sky
                 just beyond our reach . . .
It seemed as if someone was painting
                       and repainting the air
Until the day shined blankly, like a white wall.

While the teacher droned on
About positive and negative numbers
We were stilled by the absolute
                   stillness settling around us,
By the steady erasure of lawns
                   and houses across the street,
And by the hushed fragility of the trees
Glistening in the distance,
             ghostly, inhuman . . .

Our gaze moved upward against the white light,
But by the time we were released
Into the chilly, untouched
             otherness of the day

There were smudges and wingbeats
                              floating in the treetops
And a long string of footsteps—
                         the animals before us—
Crossing and criss-crossing in the snow.

Our cries shattered the stillness
                         like panes of glass
As we stomped over the playground
And lay down on our backs—
                    our spines against the earth—
To outline the figure of angels in the snow.
What joy we took in flapping our arms
                              up and down, like wings,
And sinking down lazily into the soft ground . . .

It was as if the heavens had cracked
                                   and come floating down,
And I can still remember the giddy blankness
Of lying there and looking up dazed
                         by the luminous crystals
Spiraling out of an opaque white silence . . .
But then we rose up from the ground, noisily
Brushing off our bodies,
                    and raced each other for home.

ROALD HOFFMANN

The Bering Bridge

The old men say
the sky was once so close
that if you shot an arrow up
it would bounce back at you. The sky
swallowed birds. Sometimes it lay
like the luxuriating fog
just about our tents
and a man could climb
to the opening at the top, where the smoke went out
and talk to the gods.
Then the redwoods came, sacrificing
all to the main trunk, and
they jacked up the sky,
and then men with balloons and telescopes
pushed it back further,
so it became difficult to talk straight to the gods,
one had to yell, or use the intercession of shamans.
Now I have flown myself across the Pacific,
seen the deep sky blue at 30,000 ft.
They say a man has walked on the moon.
They say the earth is getting warmer.
I see smog, the sky coming back down over California.

JONATHAN HOLDEN

Face Up

Doing leg-lifts in the field, my gaze
straight up, unchecked by anything but clouds,
it's always a slight shock to see
some high, black specks— Could they be hawks?
All over, living matter on the wing.
The sky is one, great, thriving marketplace,
its birds keep crossing.
And often a patrol of gulls,
late shoppers, quite low, the sunlight
snowy on their white cornices,
will hesitate, then circle
back and, for a minute or more,
loiter above me in the fading light,
examining this thing in throes
twitching on the ground until,
satisfied that I'm still
kicking, they wander off downwind,
and I know how the ground must always be
face up, exposed like this,
waiting to find out what the sky does next—
how it's just as you cease moving
when the sky, which had been on its way
somewhere else, pauses suddenly,
as if it might have found some use for you—
how it's only then that the world,
where we had passed so long beneath notice,
begins to take real interest in us.

September: Nederland, Colorado

Not far west of here
juts the end of the world.
The weather comes up raw
over the edge of James Peak.
Some warm days

as I cut wood I can hear
three saws or more,
hammers hurrying over a house,
battening down some distant roof.
It's just a nervous tic,
but even when the sun's strong
I'll pause to check that peak
as though a train were coming.
I know that's not
the place to look.

Up at Caribou the aspens
are out of control. They've started
to move down. As they effervesce
their banners are so bright
they hurt your eyes. Already
the destruction has arrived.
It's warm. The leaves twinkle
like pebbles under water,
they swim in unison.
No matter how steadily they swim
they're losing ground.
Days pass, one beautiful lie after another.
Our broccoli is gone.

All night rain rummages
the roof. I use my wife's abdomen
for a stove. But I can't sleep.
Somewhere in the swarming darkness
straight over our heads
the rain has stopped.
It's stiffened, white. Up there
the future starts,
so light that as it settles
on the roof it doesn't
make a sound.

Stomping with Pettit on the Battenkill

I need to whoop it up some
    and drive fast on the highways
singing to Ronstadt and Hank Williams
    loud on the tinny car stereo,
screaming like Little Richard as we whoosh by
    the roadside maples and birches,
slide-wheeling around the curves,
    ignoring all the sunburnt flag-ladies
as they try to stop us or slow us down.

I need to smoke sweet Jamaican cigars,
    puffing like an old steam engine,
screaming to the ponds and the Saabs
    and the covered bridges,
and waving at the white fronds of nimbus clouds
    passing us overhead.

I need to celebrate the first day of summer fishing
    and the easy birth of your son
and your Polaroid pictures from the hospital,
    his moist eyes and pink skin and Dara
in her gown and glamourously matted hair,
    and you in your green scrub suit
and Guy in his white cotton cap
    and his amazement.

I need to swoop down from the clouds and the antenna
    like a fat and looney bird
full of zip and Chinese food
    and great powers of exaggeration
and see water rushing over freestone beds,
    churning in frothy riffles
and languishing in green pools deep with promise
    and heavy with cannibal fish.

I need to march by a field of singing corn
    and recite Roethke and Donne and Yeats

and rave on thrashing through underbrush,
      hopping puddles and sliding down
muddy banks over slippery rock
      and wading in and feeling the cool, bronze water
press in around me, sensing the current
      washing me down to the New York line.

It's necessary to exhaust myself
      and trudge back to your truck,
fall asleep in the cab with the doors open
      and my feet sticking out
with my boots and waders still on,
      and dream about Ishmael and Agamemnon,
about Montana and the miracles of Elizabeth Bishop
      and a moose trailing us on the Henry's Fork.

I need to wake with mosquitoes humming in my ears
      and the *plink* and *pop* of trout rising
in the slick water of the pool below,
      and think about Horace
and the pleasures of country life,
      and hear the slap of your line on flat water
and the hogcalls and hoots of pleasure you make
      as if you were just born.

DAVID HUDDLE

The Snow Monkey Argues with God

Four days the mother
Snow Monkey carries
her still-born baby
before she leaves it

by a rocky stream. Then
she finds a high place
where she can brood alone
and still see her sisters

with their babies.
Four days she groomed
what should have been
as lively as these others.

If the Snow Monkey hurts
this way, can she not
also know what death is?
Or at least what it is not.

The thing she left downstream,
is not like these babies,
tugging and pulling
at their mothers, trying

to focus four-day-old
eyes on falling water
and sunlight skittering
under moving tree-branches.

While she watches her sisters
tenderly nursing
their young, she must feel
the wordless

old quarrel: better
that this paradise be burnt
to a clean white ash
than for any living

creature to have to lay down
on streamside rocks
what has been loved, what
stinks to high heaven.

Inside the Hummingbird Aviary

Thumb-sized birds in gaudy greens,
iridescent vermilions, stop
on invisible floating dimes
intricately to pivot and kiss

sugar-water bottles or desert
blossoms. Within easy snatching
distance, a Broad-billed perches,
preens, pisses in a quick squirt,

darts out a tongue half
its body length. Suddenly
suspended at breast level,
a Calliope confronts a man,

marking its possession of that
quadrant of space, the sheer force
of its watch-part heart stopping
the giant, making him laugh.

These wings are the furious
energy of perfect stillness
to make him forget kestrels
and red-masked vultures.

Here in this airy cage
he has seen five whole
hummingbirds fit
into the chambers

of his hog-sized heart.
What the man wants now
is to be desert soil
beneath a thorny bush,

the black tongues of hummers
engineering sweetness
from blossoms that once
were his body.

Perspective

This morning finches come
to my window feeder.

Sunlight sifts through
the cedar by the garage

by which a black cat
crouches, waiting.

Together this cat and I
study the finches,

I from the sofa, seeing
in sequence, window, birds,

sunlight, tree, and cat,
and cat seeing, I suppose,

beneath a veil of cedar
needles, the feeding winged

creatures that quicken
its pulse. Long seconds

we hold still, absorbed
by what we see. Then

cat inches closer,
finches fly,

and I sit with my mind
leaping, claws extended,

but winging off with every
feather still intact.

Visit of the Hawk

Across the blank blue of my study window
passed a wingspan of such consequence
that I stopped my work and sat still, certain
of something. I recall that the hairs
on the back of my neck were not standing on end.

Nevertheless:

I stood up, went straight to the skylight,
opened it and looked out, then peculiarly
knew to look back over the pitch of the roof
into the ragged green leaves and zig-zag twigs
of the butternut tree, where with savage aplomb

perched the hawk.

Urban Man Extends Head from Cockpit of House, Cranes
Neck and Observes Chicken Hawk in Butternut Tree
was the tableau, and a man with enough gumption
to have received the hawk's message that it had
come to that tree might have been expected to

understand

that the moment was purely and exclusively
just what it was, a moment, an invitation
to give over oneself to regarding the hawk.
But suddenly jittery, I began to doubt what
I plainly saw and ducked back inside to call

to my wife.

When she came upstairs, I felt this absurd relief.
Together we snuck to the skylight, poked our heads
into the airy world, and brushed against each other
most pleasantly, though of course what we saw was no
grandly feathered breast but merely a slightly

bobbing twig.

RICHARD JACKSON

The Other Day

On the other hand, to no longer wish oneself
to be everything is to put everything into
question. —Georges Bataille

I just want to say a few words about the other
day, an ordinary day I happen to recall because
my daughter has just given me a yellow flower, a buttercup,
for no reason, though it was important that other day,
that ordinary one when the stones stayed just stones
and were not symbols for anything else, when the stars made
no effort to fill the spaces we see between them,
though maybe you remember it differently, a morning
when I woke to find my hand had flowered on the breast
of my wife, a day so ordinary I happened to notice
the old woman across the street, hips so large it is
useless to try to describe them, struggle off her sofa
to pull down the shade that has separated us ever since,
her room as lonely as Keats' room on the Piazza di Spagna
where there was hardly any space for words, where I snapped
a forbidden photo that later showed nothing of his shadow
making its way to a window above Bernini's fountain,
a shadow that hesitated as if to open one of Fanny Brawne's
letters before deciding to take them to the grave unread,
who knew how little his own death must mean to the boys playing
in the Piazza below, a shadow that I later understood as
my own, indecipherable, but I just wanted to tell you about
that other day, the ordinary one, when the drunk turned over
under the local papers beneath a bush in the park, when another
in a T-shirt, tattooed, picked up the paper to check
the lottery number, then put it down, secure it was
just another ordinary day, that happy day in which
nothing left my shadow, that sorrowful day in which
nothing entered, while I took my mother to the clinic at noon
to burn away the spot on her lungs not nearly as large
as the one Keats fought, walked along the river alone,
bought broccoli for my favorite soup, and good wine,
hummed a pitiful song unconsciously, on that day
when a few million cells in each living thing died

and were replaced perfectly, when I wrote a few words,
crossed them out, wrote others, that day, I can tell you
now, when someone left a bunch of yellow flowers, buttercups,
on the grave of a nameless child burned forty years ago
in a circus fire, leaving also the child's name, Sarah,
which is why I remember that other day, because it seems
if her story could be known thousands of other ordinary days
that belonged to her might also be known, and I could tell
my daughter why I have this sudden desire to weep
all day, why I weep for the names of the dead continuing,
Samir Sayah, 16, shot in the stomach by soldiers,
Amyad Nafea, 18, shot in the chest by soldiers the moment,
perhaps, my cat scratched the door, while the cicadas
began their afternoon thrumming on that ordinary day
where I found myself powerless and guilty once again,
a day so ordinary the descendants of the very lice that bothered
Christ began their work in the hair of the boy trying
to outrun the soldiers, an ordinary day, yes, when it was
not so impossible to go looking for the dead, though
I must say that of all the deaths that inhabit me
the one the other day was the least noticed lately,
so small that I imagined myself alive all day,
holding a yellow flower, just one, just to remember,
a day I can almost forget except for its likeness to today,
a day I must call ordinary because if it is not so
ordinary then Christ, we are pitiful for our poor laments,
the deaths so small we must imagine ourselves alive all day.

For a Long Time I Have Wanted to Write a Happy Poem

> Between two worlds life hovers like a star.
> —Byron

It is not so easy to live on the earth
as an angel, to imitate the insects that dance
around the moon, to return what air we borrow
every few seconds. I am going to enter
the hour when wind dreamt of a light dress
to stroke, when water dreamt of the lips it would meet.
The famous Pascalian worm will just have to find
another heart to eat.
I will reveal the actual reason birds fly off

so suddenly from telephone wires.
The road will ask my foot for help.
The lightning will forget its thunder.
I will discover the hidden planet
to account for Pluto's eccentric orbit.
Pluto, of course, is ready to leave the alliance.
No longer will I have to lament
the death of Mary, the circus elephant,
hung with chains from a derrick on Sept. 16, 1916,
in Erwin Tennessee to punish her immortal soul
for brushing her keeper to death.
She looks out from her daguerreotype
as if she knows one day we too will hear
the stars gnaw away at our darkness.
It is not so easy.
One day I will free the clouds frozen in ponds.
No longer will the wind lose its way.
I will start hearing important voices like a real saint.
The Emir of Kuwait will answer my call.
If I am not careful I will loosen
the noose of history from around my own neck.
Just to keep sane I will have to include my weight
which is the only thing that keeps me from being a bird.
Walking on air will no longer be a problem.
Meanwhile, the Hubble telescope is still wobbling
its pictures from outer space so we will
have to rely on imagination a little longer to see clearly.
Why don't windows tell us everything they see?
Here come the characters of my sad poems.
They have been standing in line to get in
like fans for a rock concert.
They are gathering around Beatrix Potter who spent 30 years
locked in her room. The maid brings up her supper.
She sneaks out into the garden to capture
small animals to draw or reinvent before they die.
Beatrix, I say, we no longer have to kill what we see.
I know this in my heart, in my wolf, in my owl.
In the Siena of my palms. The Bergamo of my head.
In the garlic of my fingers. My friends say
I use too much. There are never enough
streets crossing the one we are stuck on.
No one wants to be a cloud anymore.
Who still believes in the transmigration of souls?

If you believe Bell's theorem, then the fact is
that the squirrel falling out of my tree this morning
makes minute sub-atomic changes from here to Australia.
Will I have to put on my pants differently now?
Just when we start to believe in moonlight
we notice how many stars it erases. It is not easy.
I am going to come back
as the birthmark on the inside of your thigh,
between your dreams of angels and solar dust,
between your drunken skirt and the one that laughs.
I am going to learn what the butterfly knows
about disguise, what so astonishes the hills.
All this is going to take constant vigilance.
In *The Last Chance Saloon*, Tombstone, Arizona,
I saw the lizard creature with its glued head,
almost human, tilted up from under the glass,
as if it didn't know which world to claim.
Apparently it fooled a lot of people in 1872.
I kept thinking if only Ovid had seen this creature
he would have known his nymphs
could never escape just by turning into trees.
In Dora Noar, Afghanistan, the young soldier,
Mohammad Anwar, age 13, believes he will turn
into a desert flower when he dies in the jihad.
The barrel of his AK-47 is sawed down
because he is as small as the four prisoners
he has returned with. They understand
that all we know of the sky we learn by listening to roots.
I was happy, he says after shooting them
against a wall, over and over again, *I was happy*.
Happy. Now maybe the earth will want to change its name.
It won't want to be the earth anymore.
Shadows will be abandoned by their objects.
The light will squander itself on the flowers
because they do not even want to be flowers anymore.
It is not easy to live on this earth.
We don't understand that the universe is
blowing away from us like litter,
but at an incredible speed.
There is a new theory that the universe is left-handed.
It has to do with the spin of quarks.
Someone else says it's in the form of a horseshoe.
The rest of the animal is metamorphosed into a black hole.

I happen to side with the fanatics who believe
it is following the call of a mythic bird too distant to see,
but this is only poetry, like the old papers
the homeless use to stuff their clothes on cold nights,
the kind of poetry that says, flowers, be happy,
trees, raise your drooping eyebrows,
sky, don't turn your back on us again,
my love, how wonderful to have lived while you lived,
which is not the sort of poetry you read anyplace anymore.

Wave

Always offshore, or already broken, gone;
Foaming around the skin;
Its print embedded in the rigid sand;
Rising from almost nothing on the beach
To show its brood of gravel,
Then coming down hard, making its point felt.

Saying, "This time I mean it. This time I will
Not have to do it over";
Repeating as if to perfect, as if,
Repeated, each were perfect; all forgotten,
One by one by one;
Every one, monster or beauty, going smash.

Wall after falling wall out to the sunset;
Or the ugly freak, capsizing
The fishing boat, reforming, riding on;
Still beautiful, lifting the frond of kelp,
Holding the silversides
Up to the eye, coming ashore in dreams.

Coming to light; invisible, appearing
To be the skeleton
Of water, or its muscle, or the look
Crossing its face; intelligence or instinct
Or neither; all we see
In substance moving toward us, all we wish for.

Already rising, lump in the throat, pulse
That taps the fingertip;
The word made flesh, gooseflesh; placid, the skin,
Remembering the sudden agitation,
Swelling again with pleasure;
All riders lifted easily as light.

Chimney Swifts

Throughout the winter, we once believed, they hid
    Nearby us, under eaves,
In nestlike thatch and thickets wedged in tile,
Sleeping as close to us as figures carved
    On vaults and open rafters.

They were, in fact, skimming the Amazon.

They are back now, with cowbirds, boat-tailed grackles,
    Kingbirds on powerlines,
And quick goldfinches heading for the fields
They drown their color in, in northern mountains.

    Swifts funnel down at twilight
Into cold flues, chattering like children.

They speak their language and we listen
    In our own, comparing them
To children, travellers, speed, and life itself,
Imparting a charmed knowledge unto us.

    To them, there are two worlds—
The soot-thick shaft and the silky bowl of sky.

To watch for them, to become expectant,
    To need their spring arrival,
To know the kink from craning back the neck
During the warm, late afternoons of April,
    Is part of the enchantment,

Is to believe they feel it, too, and act.

DONALD JUSTICE

Invitation to a Ghost

for Henri Coulette (1927–1988)

I ask you to come back now as you were in youth,
Confident, eager, and the silver brushed from your temples.
Let it be as though a man could go backwards through death,
Erasing the years that did not much count,
Or that added up perhaps to no more than a single brilliant forenoon.

Sit with us. Let it be as it was in those days
When alcohol brought our tongues the first sweet foretaste of oblivion.
And what should we speak of but verse? For who would speak of such
    things
    now but among friends?
(A bad line, an atrocious line, could make you wince: we have all
    seen it.)

I see you again turn toward the cold and battering sea.
Gull shadows darken the skylight; a wind keens among the
    chimney pots;
Your hand trembles a little.
                                What year was that?

Correct me if I remember it badly,
But was there not a dream, sweet but also terrible,
In which Eurydice, strangely, preceded *you*?
And you followed, knowing exactly what to expect, and of course she
    did turn.

Come back now and help me with these verses.
Whisper to me some beautiful secret that you remember from life.

RICHARD KENNEY

Millenary

I wish for no cars, coalfires, clang-
clang nuclear alarms, or only electric motors
for the Great Mother, and we had ten speed recycling
and aquaculture bars, and the great circle
closed again, and golden eagles eagling.
Wouldn't it be great if jobs were sweaty and outdoors
and people lived so simply nothing was lacking?
Wouldn't it be perfect if every man could hammer
his own nail and every woman hem
her own hem? And vice versa? And backpacking.
Wouldn't it be better if we could just live in harmony
with our own energy, and with nature's millennial rhythm?
O, wouldn't it be grand if there weren't too many
people in the world, and I was one of them?

Lens

Even as green summer bends
through the garden window glass,
rippling to its end in thin
isotheres somewhere over
the Gulf, where contrail snows,
where dragonfly feels wind-shear
following the hummingbird

or as the whole wrinkling star-
field's foil on some collapsed sun's
unseen, matte, prismatic curve,
where even time's tent dimples,
where atoms frail as Chinese
lanterns catch in a mind's cold
coriolis, adder's coils

closing, as the garden scene
draws close around it green glass

of the rainy window now,
so summer's wrung memory
corrects through this flint lens, love's
also, chromatic, slight, sweet
heat-shimmer, hummingbird's wings.

Concrete Delivery Delayed by Goose & Gosling Crossing, Late March, Mallett's Bay

OK, right here's the first dry pavement geyser-
ing a slow New England spring: zinc culverts
hooosh, margins marshes, ditches moats, toads' argots
smirching the gusty winds and sloughs where birds mince
wordless through reflected clouds, and here, in vertical
file, *strut, slap*, this goose and nine piddling goslings
intersect the dotted centerline, where clemency
comes down with the clutch in the sky-high cab, diesel
manifold gargling tuning forks in the ugly lingos
of big trucks, hot stack puffing up another silty
heaven over slow revolutions, loose cement
sliding, sliding, sliding its wet drum sling,
and nothing in the whole world hard or straight
but the driver's eye and the goose's gait.

MAXINE KUMIN

October, Yellowstone Park

How happy the animals seem just now,
all reading the sweetgrass text, heads down
in the great yellow-green sea of the high plains—
antelope, bison, the bull elk and his cows

moving commingled in little clumps, the bull
elk bugling from time to time his rusty screech
but not yet in rut, the females not yet in heat,
peacefully inattentive—the late fall

asters still blooming, the glacial creeks running clear.
What awaits them this winter—which calves will starve
to death or driven by hunger stray from the park
to be shot on the cattle range—they are unaware.

It is said that dumb beasts cannot anticipate
though for terror of fire or wolves some deep
historical memory clangs out of sleep
pricking them to take flight. As flight pricked the poet

dead seventeen years today, who for seventeen
years before that was a better sister
than any I, who had none, could have conjured.
Dead by her own hand, who so doggedly whined

at Daddy Death's elbow that the old Squatter
at last relented and took her in. Of sane mind
and body aged but whole I stand by the sign
that says we are halfway between the equator

and the North Pole. Sad but celebratory
I stand in full sun on the 45th parallel
bemused by what's to come, by what befell,
by how our friendship flared into history.

Fair warning, Annie, there will be no more
elegies, no more direct-address songs

conferring the tang of loss, its bitter flavor
as palpable as alum on the tongue.

Climbing up switchbacks all this afternoon,
sending loose shale clattering below,
grimly, gradually ascending to a view
of snowcaps and geysers, the balloon

of Old Faithful spewing, I hear your voice
beside me (you, who hated so to sweat!)
cheerfully cursing at eight thousand feet
the killers of the dream, the smalltime advice-

laden editors and hangers-on. I've come
this whole hard way alone to an upthrust slate
above a brace of eagles launched in flight
only to teeter, my equilibrium

undone by memory. I want to fling
your cigarette- and whiskey-hoarse chuckle
that hangs on inside me down the back wall
over Biscuit Basin. I want the painting

below to take me in. My world that threatened
to stop the day you stopped, faltered
and then resumed, unutterably altered.
Where wildfires crisped its hide and blackened

whole vistas, new life inched in. My map
blooms with low growth, sturdier than before.
Thus I abstain. I will not sing, except
of the elk and his harem who lie down in grandeur

on the church lawn at Mammoth Hot Springs,
his hatrack wreathed in mist. This year's offspring
graze in the town's backyards, to the dismay
of tenants who burst out to broom them away.

May the car doors of tourists slam, may cameras go wild
staying the scene, may the occasional
antelope slip into the herd, shy as a child.
May people be ravished by this processional.

May reverence for what lopes off to the hills
at dusk be imprinted on their brain pans
forever, as on mine. As you are, Anne.
All of you hammered golden against the anvil.

The Fish Pond

Not full of fish—that's imprecise—but full.
Too much so: frogs and newts,
              prolix wrigglers. Small. Dull.
And yet they drew to the scummed September surface
a single osprey, of one mind, acute.
              As talons pierced the water, wings shone wet,
a visitor's vision of his own life's purpose
(fragmentary, qualified,
              jerry-rigged with age like anybody's)
seemed worse than mere impediment.
It seemed beneath contempt.
              He's always moved by hawks that dive

to disremembered dream: To strike directly.
The broadleaves, moribund, will drop.
              When school let out his children dropped
their books amid the mudroom's p.m. clutter:
ballgloves, rucksacks, dust-fluff on the tile.
              A local government official's smile
smeared page one of the evening paper.
Though many loves live blessedly
              at home, he came away alone, out here.
But it returns so fast, the banal—
the pond's again a turmoil
              of squirming things; and somehow riled,

the Touch-Me-Not explodes its pods on shore,
breeze broadcasting countless seed.
              Hard to bear in mind, one bird,
its solitary shriek and plunge, its grip.
He kneels down on this strip of beach to plead,
              vaguely and quaintly upward, Hear me, Hear.
But is it *to* or *from* some One
that he presumes to wish a word?
              It seemed the fish-hawk knew at once to prey
and, rising in the instant, slip

not out of sight alone
        but even sound: two foxes yip

down here in someone's orchard, north, close by;
there's hissing homebound traffic, southward;
        somewhere, a hoot-and-clucky clamor
of fattening hens and geese as dusk sneaks east.
He's bound to all of this by nature, sense—
        sand's damp on his sore knees, that huff of breeze
paws at his neck and bears him scents
of surfeit too: of mouldered hay,
        of grainfields' cloying germ and ear and tassle,
of methane, deadfall, mossy stones
washed to myriad forms
        by streams from five surrounding swamps,

their weed- and root-growth thick as hair on cattle.
Now lesser beasts inside their warrens
        prepare for random ambulations,
crepuscular and timid: worthy victims,
each beneath contempt . . . though what is *he*?
        What is a man who'd kneel these hours away,
longing to strike or else be stricken?
Such imprecision. Hear, he mumbles,
        as a Corn Moon stains the humpback mountains,
as a thousand shadows clog the meadow,
as a thousand creatures stir,
        as stars in ragged herds mull in the sky

where he beheld one fierce hawk, sleek on air.

Prospect

for Don Metz at 50

As we raised our tent—in the winter firmament, it seemed—
        The Hedgehog Den shone.
        Why Hedgehog Den?
        Why ask? It had its name

From before we ever dreamed to speak it. Like Pickledish, say,
        Or Holt's or Tinkhamtown,

Rat-Away,
Hardscrabble. Loud, unknowing,

We'd echo such words off granite and ice, less greedy for meanings
Back then than for savor of sound
Under each round moon.
We two were thirty and some.

Grease was in our skillet, booze in cold tin cups,
Things that in time we learned
Were bad for us.
Still, the prospect was fine,

There couldn't be any doubt: To our south, the lower creatures
Dozed under mud in the pond,
And predators coursed
Its frost-bedazzled beaches,

Enviable, airborne. North, from a pinetop, gusts flicked forth
Snow like a nacreous rain
In the young-year shine.
Above us and off to eastward,

Swaddled by cloud, it seemed, in every season and weather,
Smart's Mountain's schisted dome,
Vaguely divine
Somehow, although we'd been there.

Andromeda, westerly, stared at the river. Our prospect as well
Was down, as we couldn't have known,
Intent on a fall
Out of her constellation:

A plummeting *up* of stars, like our white-plumed conversation's,
To galaxies unseen
Where spirit could join them,
Surely, and even body,

Full though it may have been of quiet, of unknown poisons,
Wrapped though it were in down,
In wools and furs.
Sky, as they say, was the limit.

Another limit looms, and now the bright loud words
        Set deeper back in our minds:
        Moody, Demmick,
        Dunbar's, Cottonstone.

We thought they'd live forever, and so we feel a shiver—
        More than we used to, friend,
        Blood pumping,
        Hot, the cookfire-tinder's

Flume of spark in gravity's spite upwinging;
        To think that even the land's
        Ghosts may surrender!
        What at last will remain?

Well, it wasn't—was it?—the ghostly we sought in our old prospects.
        Or if it was, Things change.
        Whatever else,
        While I chase you into fifty,

What in heaven would a clod like me articulate
        As retrospective theme?
        Real estate,
        The country now, and we

These days between us almost describe a century.
        I pray they'll keep ever on,
        The talk and laughter.
        But I'll say another name.

Now that our outlook's nearer—dark of the moon,
        Cycle searching an end—
        And sounds go quieter,
        The memories may ascend.

But Love, earthbound, is firmer. And surer the prospect, and keener.

Paternity

He waves his breakfast knife and screams he'll kill me.
Old mitigations—
he's hungry, tired, his pain and fury

have nothing to do
with me, will pass into nothing—
pass into nothing, my flight to reason

failing against these morning shrieks
that augur murder.
He slams the door, the very lath of the ceiling

quakes, and a precious print that now means nothing
tilts on its tack. The boy is my son.
The print is a Hopper,

Night Shadows: a man
crosses from dark to dark through uncertain light,
unspeakably alone.

The boy has hiked his socks, his short pants sag,
so that only the cap
of his knee still shows, abraded by play, or might

still show if he'd stayed.
The knee becomes a pink epitome
of all I desire: dumb, rapt,

I stare at a door.
And then, *tweet-tweet*, I imitate the birds
outside, that the child may hear and judge me

not indifferent, but not inclined
(though it's a lie)
to over-value the stab of impassioned words.

I whistle to be
translated—that suddenly seeming the burden
of life, long life, damned long life—

to show another side. Let him assume
again my mind,
like my flesh and blood, I think, as equally sudden,

coffee water leaps from spout to burner,
its mists and hisses
portending the inner clouds and windy sounds

of a place where I'll fall
and be flogged by the wing of doubt, by dream's wing,
and predatory Eros's.

I *will* the fall,
as one might choose to welcome the coming of migraine:
better than nothing, that chill in the skin

of the left-hand thumb,
the numbing tongue, the shadow-sight,
twitch of nerve and muscle along the jawline.

Now something flashes
upon that inward eye that is the horror
of solitude: only a silly bike,

its Reelfur coontails flapping from handgrips,
and I astride.
A door has banged. Behind me, the calls of my father,

then tuneless whistles. Starling. Cowbird. Jay.
There's a shadow or fog
ahead, toward which I glide:

cloud in which our earthly cries must end,
I think, and think,
Damned short as well as long.

I want to fly back,
to the cup we bought for a joke at that tourist trap
with its sunrise scene, calm, pink

flamingoes wading through its maudlin inscription;
coffee; a household, sweet, foursquare;
belled cat on the lip

of the worn-wood kitchen counter, yawning;
the woman who for all our parenthood
lies ripe as pears

in autumn, stored behind closed doors.
I long to lay a soothing
hand on the blood-

and grass-stained knee of the boy
who chokes and sobs.
And so in my need to imagine something

against the fog, I summon the image
of a mourning dove
who flies backlit in mind across

the sun, is dark,
a dagger: a side, I'll say; of peace.
Dark dagger, but still a dove.

Peace, or its winged partner, love.

DAVID LEHMAN

Greenhouses and Gardens

It began as an item on a questionnaire
Filled out by anxious high school seniors.
The wise daughter was expected to elect
The grassy knoll inside the mind and reject
The bright green astroturf in the domed stadium
Where fraternity boys play solitaire.

Then it was the title of the book she did not write
About the garden of Eden and the greenhouse effect.
The garden of Eden turned out to be a gnarled apple tree
With a double trunk in a far corner of Iraq.
Our primal parents, expelled from paradise, proceed
By stages to acid rain, global warming, ozone loss.

What happens next was predictable perhaps:
They become beggars in the kingdom of greed.
"Adam and Eve on a raft, wreck 'em and give 'em oars,"
Cries the counterman to the cook, closing the book.
But the eye of the observer remains on the fruit
Of that forbidden tree, where nature and human nature meet.

A natural wilderness awaits the veteran time-traveler,
Who must describe the place before she enters it:
Is it a desert or a tropical rain forest? Men come
And take her to the land of metaphor, where biblical grapes
The size of melons grow, or to that other place,
Where the retired warden sits, wrapped in blankets,

In a greenhouse with a solar heating panel on the roof,
Watching a younger man wipe the sweat off his neck
With his handkerchief. They are having a debate.
It is clear that the warden's idea of paradise
Is the moonlit arbor where he saw *As You Like It*
As a student in Oxford. "But gardens are as man-made

As greenhouses are," counters the younger man,
Whose bower of bliss is a bedroom without walls.

Exposing the fallacies of both positions,
You came along on a cold dismal April morning
With your vision of the dead returning from the earth
To compete with the living for sunlight and space.

On the Nature of Desire

1.

There are, said my old philosophy professor, two kinds
Of people in the world: those who divide everything in two
And those who don't. At the dinner party, Janice was talking

About computers. IBMs are masculine, she said. Macintoshes
Are feminine. That's exactly what some people say
About art and nature, said her husband, Don. Do you really

Believe that, asked Mark. I mean, should hurricanes be named
After women, as in the old days, and is the construction of a city
The quintessential male act, Nature subdued by Apollo's merry men?

2.

Nature, then, is the great eruption—flood, earthquake,
Tidal wave, volcano—that interrupts the World Series
And sends men running to their cars and their private visions

Of sublime waterfalls in the early nineteenth century when
Man could feel alone in a benevolent universe whose god
Was not an almighty moralist but the outburst of an imagination

Capable of anything. Nature is the calamity that overwhelms man
With terror yet draws him into it, and he creeps to the edge
Of the canyon, holding the hand of the woman he loves.

3.

The laws governing isosceles triangles do not apply
To man, wife and child. The professor of mathematics is one
Of two men in love with the same woman. The other is his son

By a previous mistress. Both are fearless.
They know that nature is a woman, a forest on fire
That can't stop burning. The goal is not to quench the fire

But to let it burn. The dancing around the fire goes on
All night, and the victorious couple is the last
To drop down exhausted and consummate their love.

4.

I saw her again this evening. She had the face of the woman
With the braided hair at the desk in the public library,
Where she used to work before she grew up and I moved away.

When I got up close I could tell how young she was—maybe 17,
The age we were when we met. I was reading *The Sun Also Rises*
And she walked over, brought me a pile of books about Hemingway,

And let her hand linger on mine, accidentally brushed.
Neither of us understood the nature of our desire,
Just that it was mutual. Our ignorance fed the fire.

5.

In those days you could have a girl in your dormitory room
Twice a month, on Saturday night, from seven in the evening
Until one a.m. The lights were out, but the dust of my window

Caught the glare of a streetlamp and the reflection of a neon
"Chop Suey" sign. An imaginary wind lifted her skirt,
And she smiled, letting me look. "You know, you could be expelled

For this." She had theories: she was Catholic, I was Jewish.
She was ashamed of her breasts, I was proud of my poems.
The antitheses were alluring in the early morning light.

6.

There are those who insist that all differences except
The biological are trivial and that the oppositions
Between Apollo and Dionysus, nature and culture and so on,

Are all of them sentimental and false, because they concern
Only the man and the woman, neglecting the third who walks always
Beside them. The great mystery is time and how we lost it

And cannot get it back, cannot convert memory into action,
The slim-breasted girl in the public library; can barely recall
The face in the photograph, the body beneath my own.

7.

Man in the state of nature was unalienated from his labor
Or in a state of constant warfare with his fellow primates.
They fought over an ordinary woman in an ordinary bar,

As if the fear of death didn't matter. The survivor wins her.
She is convinced he has put her on a pedestal in order
To look up her skirt: once a philosopher, twice a pervert.

Watching the couple's antics in bed are his mother and father,
Her mother and father, and the Marquis de Sade.
The son, asleep in the next room, is guarded by angels.

8.

In summer camp, the girl knows that any partner,
However unappealing, is better than no partner at all,
So she agrees to dance with him, a slow dance, an awkward waltz,

And when the torture is over, and their bodies separate,
He is shocked at what he sees: "Your dress is bleeding."
The boy becomes a man when his desire distracts him

From his fear, and he cannot resist the return to her womb
Though it rhymes with death at every orifice. The dress
Is put on to be taken off, the bed made to be undone.

9.

Why, then, is this city full of randy men, anxious
To cheat on their wives, and lonely women, who learned to say no
To importunate suitors long ago? If the scholars of sex

Are right, every Eve defends herself against her own desire
While trying to allay Adam's fear. If the poets of sex
Are right, the exchange of body fluids is a function

Of natural thirst, and love is the speechless joy
That lasts until it dies, and the couple close their eyes,
Tired, unashamed, nude and asleep for their hour together.

GARY MARGOLIS

Autumn Bees on Broccoli Blossoms Gone-by

Now the honey flow is over
    and the bees will want to go
down into their deepest boxes,

    to feed on their surer food,
not forgetting the first blossoms
    can't begin here before May.

The bee keeper brings
    his jars of sugar water
to put under each hive's outer

    cover, so a hungry bee can draw
at will off his preparation.
    Even with this free, steady fix,

a few fly out toward the frost-
    killed gardens searching for
semblances of flowers, because

    for them, it seems, even color
is a sweet remembrance. It's common
    to find bees nursing all day

on a dead broccoli blossom
    and to want to tell them all
to go home. But there are no words

    for the beauty of this perfect
disappointment, for the arrangement
    of feeling between these patients

and their ill-chosen cures.
    Once they have gotten their fill
of clinging, of nursing on

the flower's empty chambers,
they can lift off, lighter than
    when they landed and full of enough

yellow light to last them until May,
    when a new blossom will bring them
back out of autumn's morphine hive.

On the Way to the Sitter's

I could take you by the orchards
    and still skirt the duster's spray.
That way's shortest and we could
    watch apples weigh down their
branches with their own sweet weight.
    I'd say the apples grew partly
because of the rain and wait to tell
    you the biting spray tells each fruit
how red to turn and when it's time
    to drop into a Jamaican's hand.
I could take you another way,
    past the church and Longey's store,
by the roadside houses that display
    their home-made signs. I'd ask if you
saw the one for lamb, its hand-
    painted sheep grazing next to their
shepherd's address, saw the work
    clothes swaying from our neighbor's
lines like chicory when the wind
    from a truck or the wind drives by.
I could take you the way you ask for,
    which is always just out-of-the-way,
past the house with paper lanterns
    strung and every car the owners drove
parked next to the white machines
    that worked for them, they want
to see turn red on their own.
    They raise a pair of baby bulls
each of you could walk, steering them
    with the hair of a willow switch,

nearly the way the young oxherder
    tamed his ox in the six drawings Jitoku
drew of love inside of mind. I think of him
    each time I go this way, so we can stop
and pick some overhanging, roadside
    Macs to rub the spray from,
we can see our faces curving on
    their skin, before we disappear by biting in.

Kicking and Breathing

I need the walls on either end,
    so I can turn and push off
into the pool's deeper water.
    The Cape's pilot whales are

running themselves aground again,
    as if they didn't know a beach
or the Great Reef is their wall.
    All explanation fails for why

they are found gasping there
    in the receding tide, and
why those volunteers wade out
    among the herd to hold one,

to see which ones can be turned
    around, pushed back.
I think I can let myself know
    one whale wants to die,

but thinking somehow
    they wish this as a group,
and then turn in together,
    turns my lunchtime swimming

friends into a horrible
    team. It's swimmers in
both lanes beside me—kicking
    and breathing—on days I want

to beach myself, I imitate.
   I take their strokes as mine,
breathing in what they breathe
   out. Three whales, I heard, were

dragged out in a net, before
   the veternarian's needle could
keep them still. They must need
   to practice death before they

die, and without dreams or a way
   to write their lives, unpiloted,
they head in, their own small
   city thrashing the sea, grinding

their bellies on the unwelcome sand,
   unable to feel a wall at the end
of their Atlantic lane, to count a lap's
   exhaled, unbroken breaths.

PAUL MARIANI

Landscape with Dog

Often up the back steps he came
bearing gifts: frozen squirrels,
sodden links of sausage, garter snakes,
the odd sneaker. The gnarled marks
are still there as witness that,
confined, he took his tensions out
on doors & tables. And life went on,
& mornings, peace & war, good times
& depressions. Pale sticks turned
to trees, boys to larger boys, then men.
Icestorms, wakes, elections came & went.
And always he was there, like air,
a good wife. But then there's this
to think about & think about again:

the last time I saw Sparky he was dying.
His legs trembled & he kept moping
after me. I remember trying to get
my stubborn mower started, with no time
then to stop & pet a dog. And having
no time left himself, Sparky
thanked me in the only way he could
for eleven years of care, then got up
& walked out of my life & lay down
somewhere in the woods to die,
one of the best things life ever
handed me, while I went on looking
for a one-inch nut & bolt
in among my rusting odds & ends.

Shadow Portrait

In the lost portrait by Siqueiros,
the face lifts like a death's head
from the shadows. White hair & blotched,

disfigured skin. The bruised lips
more an aging madame's than a man's,

the eyes sewn shut as if in prayer.
It is only 32, this face,
but like Villon's it knows, in spite of
whatever lies he feeds it, it cannot last
another year. Hiss of scorpions on the sands

at nightfall, hiss of seabeached turtles,
the waves advancing and retreating.
He strains to hear it all, as if somehow
he might fathom. It is not, he sees,
that what he looks at hard looks hard

back at him. Things hide themselves, hold
still, then spit their sibilants back
into his face . . . Bougainvillea
& the banyan tree, palms aflame
with the firefeathered forms of avocets,

the bronze bells of Easter morning blooming.
This the vouchsafed ecstasy of vision.
This & the boy he had there on the dusty floor
at Taxco. Then self-exile, the benzined waters
north of Cuba, the whirr of circling fins.

Beneath his fastened lids he watches
as the brilliance of the billowing sails
lose their light & turn back into empty
sheets of paper. He knows now that, wherever
he is going, there is no way he can make it.

Moonrise as Abstraction

Last night, driving west along the parkway
towards the hospital, he watched the harvest moon
lift itself like an old man above the treeline.

The oncoming lights blurred large & ominous,
whirred past, then curved away. Bare branches
stretched their twisted fingers upward, black

etched black against the silver black. He knew
his friend was dying. The pockmarked craters
of the pallid moon looked down. There was

a grinding in the going round of wheels, a weight,
a gravity, as up rushed the hypnotic lights
to meet him. Except for the preternatural

brilliance of his eyes, his friend would be
the shadow only of his former self,
the waning of a light which for a time

had seemed to rise above the other lights around,
a light egyptian, regal, unlike the common string
of traffic still approaching, yet for a little

while closer than the cold and distant stars.
In the darkened room there at the hospital,
his friend's gaze would be fixed upon the ballgame,

as if it mattered anymore who won or lost,
when all that mattered was that where
his friend was going he knew he could not follow,

though he'd prayed as he had never prayed before
to keep him from his too-soon leaving
on his final journey west. But then the moon

shook free of the branches like the solitary
king it is, and his hands unclenched & bid adieu,
as if now his friend could ease him on his way.

Mountain View with Figures

As if Cézanne had rendered it: a palimpsest
of planes, a dreamscape realized, an imbrication,
the easel facing the brilliant south exposure.

In the middle foreground a patch of shadowed gulley.
Beyond: a swirl of crosshatched pines. He counts again
the colors: a tan, a green, a gray, a tan, a tan.

Beyond the graygreen strokes he feels the Absolute
malignly beckon in the bald & treeless peaks.
He stares now as he contemplates his stony labors,

the hissing hesitations he knows must lie ahead.
It is this that has kept him sleepless night after
night: fear teetering on the edge of the abyss,

empty speculations deep enough for even an Empedocles.
He knows the most he has to paint with
is a round of absinthe sounds & acrobatic stanzas.

Those and a syntax even the boys at the Sorbonne
could nod assent to. He wants the words to paint
his naked canvas, words to ring in the Final Absolute

at last. He wants to feel it is enough. He wants to shout
& hear the mountain ring. If he climbed it now
he would at least expect to find himself transfigured.

Variations on a Theme by Justice

Miami sunlight, as in a painting
by the poet Donald Justice:
a V of three pelicans drifting south
past the condos and the royal palms,
aflame now with the green scent
of coconut & parrot. Out, out
towards the darker waters
the pelicans keep drifting . . .

I watch my in-laws, both eighty now,
shift about their small apartment
here north of the city, and guess
at what it is they must be thinking:
the brilliance of some perfect noon,
the doctor staring down into the shallows
of their eyes, as the soul slips now
through the gaping fissures . . .

It is what we always think about,
though we mask it any way we can . . .
to think instead of sunlight in Miami,
as in a painting by the poet Donald
Justice, which shows the keylime
cobalt brilliance of a surging
Gulf Stream, and in the background
three dots drifting slowly out to sea . . .

for Donald Justice

Reflections after a Dry Spell

> *A good poet is someone who manages, in a*
> *lifetime of standing out in thunderstorms, to be*
> *struck by lightning five or six times.*
> *—Randall Jarrell*

And the one that took this literally
Is the one that you still sometimes see
In the park, running from tree to tree

On likely days, out to stand under
The right one *this* time—until the thunder
Rebukes him for yet another blunder. . . .

But the one who knew it was nothing more
(That flash of lightning) than a metaphor,
And said as much, as he went out the door—

Of that one, if you're lucky, you just may find
The unzapped verse or two he left behind
On the confusion between World and Mind.

What the Dark Proposes

—But no, it isn't over for them yet:
They sit off by themselves, watching the sun set
    Behind the hills striated now with fog.
Two coffees, one forbidden cigarette:

They pass at intervals its glowing coal
From each to other. Pressed sheets of fog roll
    Into the valley right before the ridge
Of hills like mountains in a Chinese scroll,

Where fog is something dreamt of by the ocean
Beyond those hills: an invisible commotion
    Of large and little waves all pressing shoreward,
Quietly dispersing in slow motion

A few last tattered bits of marked-down light:
But this the hills had kept out of their sight.
    Seeing beyond them was beyond them both,
Who saw no further than the coming night,

A room that would be there as certainly
As was the ocean which they could not see:
    And in that room, all they would first remember
And afterwards imagine, when memory

Would no more lift a fingertip to trace
The contours of a now-forgotten face,
    The gestures that imperceptibly once led
Into the fierce constrictions of embrace:

Persistence of the gestures that renew
Desire is the legend woven through
    Those days and nights, now to be read only
Here in what I have written of these two,

Who sit where I have put them and think about
The way it goes from certainty to doubt
    And back again until the coffee's cold
And the glowing coal is carefully stubbed out.

They leave tomorrow, taking what is theirs.
A sky magnificently shot with stars
    Has been arranged tonight to bring them in
Just as the last slip of sunlight disappears

Beyond the hills: and while coyotes howl
Their heartsick threnodies, a Great Horned Owl
    Gives answers to the questions that she poses,
Another hungry feeder on the prowl.

WILLIAM MATTHEWS

Names

Ten kinds of wolf are gone and twelve of rat
and not a single insect species.
Three sorts of skink are history and two
of minnow, two of pupfish, ten of owl.
Seventeen kinds of rail are out of here
and five of finch. It comforts us to think
the dinosaurs bought their farms all at once,
but they died at a rate of one species
per thousand years. Life in a faster lane
erased the speckled dace, the thicktail chub,
two kinds of thrush and six of wren, the heath
hen and Ash Meadows killfish. There are four
kinds of sucker not born any minute
anymore. The Christmas Island musk shrew
is defunct. Some places molt and peel so fast
it's a wonder they have any name:
the Chatham Island bellbird flew the coop
as did the Chatham Island fernbird, the
Lord Howe Island fantail and the Lord Howe
Island blackbird. The Utah Lake sculpin,
Arizona jaguar and Puerto
Rican caviomorph, the Vegas Valley
leopard frog and New Caledonian lorikeet?
They've hit the road for which there is no name
a mouth surrounds so well as it did theirs.
The sea mink's crossed the bar and the great auk's
ground time here was brief. Four forms the macaw
took are cancelled checks. Sad Adam fills his lungs
with haunted air, and so does angry Eve:
they meant no name they made up for farewell.
They were just a couple starting out,
a place they could afford, a few laughs,
no champagne but a bottle of rosé.
In fact Adam and Eve are not their names.

The Bear at the Dump

Amidst the too much that we buy and throw
away and the far too much we wrap it in
the bear found a few items of special
interest—a honeydew rind, a used tampon,
the bone from a leg of lamb. He'd rock back
lightly onto his rear paws and slash
open a plastic bag, and then his nose—
jammed almost with a surfeit of rank
and likely information, for he would pause—
and then his whole dowsing snout would
insinuate itself a little way
inside. By now he'd have hunched his weight
forward slightly, and then he'd snatch it back,
trailed by some tidbit in his teeth. He'd look
around. What a good boy am he.
The guardian of the dump was used
to this and not amused. "He'll drag that shit
every which damn way," he grumbled
who'd dozed and scraped a pit to keep that shit
where the town paid to contain it.
The others of us looked and looked. "City
folks like you don't get to see this often,"
one year-round resident accused me.
Some winter I'll bring him down to learn
to love a rat working a length of subway
track. "Nope," I replied. Just then the bear
decamped for the woods with a marl of grease
and slather in his mouth and on his snout,
picking up speed, not cute (nor had he been
cute before, slavering with greed, his weight
all sunk to his seated rump and his nose stuck
up to sift the rich and fetid air, shaped
like a huge, furry pear), but richly
fed on the slow-simmering dump, and gone
into the bug-thick woods and anecdote.

The Dogs of Montone

Jockeyed by fleas and led, as we say
in lazy contempt of fellow humans,
by the nose, that spy par excellence, they
are the book that could be filled
by what they do not know. With what
they do know, you could fill a town.
People, too, coil down like water

through the spiralled streets to the piazza,
the basin of the town. The dogs
that aren't asleep or being fed
snuffle along the uric stones.
The San Francesco bells sound
8:15 and the valley,
trough of a thousand shades

of green, begins cooly to fill
with dusk. The sun, blood orange
at the last, subsides like a toy
boat in flames. The first streetlights buzz on
and bats unfurl. Two or three dogs,
like raddled islands, bark: the lake
of the black night is everywhere.

Sentence

Bloated and mesmerized by raspberries,
the possum wobbled into the open
like a blinking child come out to the sun
from an afternoon movie, and because
time takes no time in a poem, I can hear
the guns bray and smell the spattered bowels
and fermented berries, I can hold
my hands like wafers athwart my ears,
I can feel like a fog in my nostrils
the sudden, fragrant compost, half-shit, half-
food, all memory, though I was too young
to remember much but the future, one
death, one fiesta, sweet stench like a flag,
one possum at a time and the vast fields.

The Rented House in Maine

At dawn, the liquid clatter of rain
pocks the bay and stutters on the roof.
Even when it's this gray, the first slant light
predicts across the rug gaunt shadows
of the generic paper birds
my landlord's pasted to the eastern wall,

all glass, to fend specific birds
from bonking themselves dull or worse
against the bright blare of false sky.
From the bay the house must look
like a grade-school homeroom gussied up
for parents' night. I like to build

a small fire first thing in the morning,
drink some coffee, drive to town,
buy the *Times*, drive back to embers
the color of canned tomato soup
(not made with water but with milk).
In this house I fell—no, dove—

in love, and elsewhere, day by day,
it didn't last. Tethered to lobster traps,
buoys wobble on the bay. On the slithering
surface of the water, the rain seems
to explode—chill shrapnel, and I look
away. Embers and cool coffee. Matter,

energy, the speed of light: the universe
can be explained by an equation. Everything
that goes from one side of the equal sign
is exactly replaced from the other; i.e.,
nothing much happens at a speed so fast
we scarcely notice it, but so steadily

the math always checks out. This is thought
as I know and love it. Why did that marriage
fail? I know the reasons and count the ways.
The clouds with squalls in their cheeks,
like chaws or tongues, have broken up.
The fire is down, the coffee cold, the sun is up.

Chott

Through the tentflap, across the air mattress, up over my
    shoulderblade,
The blindfold of sunlight slips into place. On your borrowed Walkman

The muezzin's morning call to prayer clears its throat of unbelief.
Already out there pillars of sand are forming to hold up the sky

For minutes at a time before they buckle and collapse with exhaustion.
One more day on the salt flats. Air tight as a water-skin. Black flies

On your eyelid. Sun. Two suns, the counterfeit sun curling like a petal,
Separating from the true, wrenched from it to simmer on its reflection,

A hand's breadth between them now, the true one hauled up dripping.
Whose idea was a week on a dead sea anyway? A week away from
    the port,

Away from the café's chewed pits and prawnshuck, the
    featheredged kef.
In their teaching rooms, the holy men were promising *He has forced*

The night and the day into your service, set forgiving mountains down
Lest the earth should move away with you. Caked mud and
    brine crust,

Like two drops of blood on a pillow, both dried to the same
    charred brick.
To brush away those flies risks touching you. The Jeep hood flutters.

Out beyond your head, slumped now over your breasts, the horizon's
Hit on the day's first mirage—lolling palms, a milky water hole,

Two Frenchmen in rockers. Is that a woman, her arm up to shade
    her eyes?
Or protect herself? A bronze basin over—(*Wake up, damn you!*
    Wake. Up.)

A mirage, the goatherd said, is always something you once had or
   wanted.
So by that logic, the past . . . no matter. It was only another promise.

Remember those first days in bed? The braided candlelight, the net
   of stars,
The shadow-drawn streams running underneath the body, under the
   loathing.

The years, the miles out and back are run through us, just sitting here.
This whole thing, it's inside a bottle, that empty fifth Hussein kept

His miniature desert in for the tourists, the dwarfed ruins he'd
   tweezered
Onto a dirty inch of nowhere, the how many layers of wornaway rock,

The grains of lives dry as the world's bone. Look at the sun in there,
That glistening drop of poison at the tip of the scorpion's tail.

Late Night Ode

Horace, IV.i

It's over, love. Look at me pushing fifty now,
   Hair like grave-grass growing in both ears,
The piles and boggy prostrate, the hanged man's penis,
   The sour taste of each day's first lie,

And that recurrent dream of years ago pulling
   A swaying bead-chain of moonlight,
Of slipping between the cool sheets of dark
   Along a body like my own, but blameless.

What good's my cut-glass conversation now,
   Now I'm so effortlessly vulgar and sad?
You get from life what you can shake from it?
   For me, it's g and t's all day and CNN.

Try the blond boychick lawyer, entry level
   At eighty grand, who pouts about the overtime,
Keeps Evian and a beeper in his locker at the gym,
   And hash in tinfoil under the office fern.

There's your hound from heaven, with buccaneer
    Curls and perfumed war-paint on his nipples.
His answering machine always has room for one more
    Slurred, embarrassed call from you-know-who.

Some nights I've laughed so hard the tears
    Won't stop. Look at me now. Why *now*?
I long ago gave up pretending to believe
    Anyone's memory will give as good as it gets.

So why these stubborn tears? And why do I dream
    Almost every night of holding you again,
Or at least of diving after you, my long-gone,
    Through the bruised unbalanced waves.

CHRISTOPHER MERRILL

Day Lilies: Instructions and an Elegy

for Robert Jebb (1944–1990)

Plant them with shadows in mind, under a dying
Cottonwood, in a bed of bone meal and arrowheads.
Lather the soil with humus or Apache tears
—The drops of sleek obsidian culled from the creek
Below the slumbering volcano. Use the tools
—A spading fork, a trough—of the illiterate
Day laborer who studies numerology
And cannot count; like him, you must work in the dark.
Thus wake and bathe before sunrise on the Day of the Dead;
Gather supplies—a burlap sack, a bone-shaped loaf
Of bread, death's-heads to hang from every door; then wait.
At nightfall dig the flowers from a roadside ditch.
Hum no dirges while you divide the clumps; only
Waltzes will do. Pray for the pilgrims killed last Easter
Marching to a church built on sacred land: the blessed
Dirt that lured them to that shrine, that might have healed
Their relatives' infirmities—a limp, or fading
Vision, or infertility—may save your transplants
From the flash floods and droughts that score and scorch this canyon.
Cover the roots with charms against mule deer and dogs.
Then count, O count next June the short-lived blooms—the yellow
Swans preening in the sun, then disappearing at dusk;
The blaring lemon trumpets no one listens to;
The orange bells that ring now for the hummingbird
And not for you, my friend, who might have planted them.

The Bees

After a bear ransacked their hive, strewing wood, wax,
And honey over grass, and rabbitbrush, and asters,
Trampling worm-eaten apples and a peach tree bending
Into the earth, arming the orchardist who loathed
Nocturnal creatures more than an early snow,—the bees

Tunneled through twigs and leaves, stones and tar, burrowing
Into the roof, then ceiling of a house—an estate
The absent owners wouldn't visit, settle, or seize.

Around the queen they wintered in the insulation;
And on the first warm day of spring they fell from the rafters
Into the living room, a snowpack severing
Its hold on a hillside, then flooded over walls
Of photographs, last year's phone book, throw rags and shag,
Buzzing the dusty windows and a dying jasmine,
To cluster on the sun-raked sill, prepared to gather
Pollen and nectar from the flowers still outside.

When snowmelt swelled the creek and irrigation ditch,
And the trees whitened, like a ring of moons revolving
Around the orchard, and the bear stirred in its den
High on the mesa overlooking that estate,
The orchardist loaded his gun, then hid at dusk
Among his falling blossoms, the squall of lights the owners
Had never seen. Inside, the phone rang. Stopped. Lamps glowed.
The bees swarmed the locked doors, fireplace screen, floor. The house
    hummed.

JOHN FREDERICK NIMS

Understanding the Universe

We're told how the great mazy world we wander
Was once a cozy garden we could tend:
Clouds snug above; the sun, the moon up yonder
Distant a piece, but neighborly, a friend.
But now, since Galileo—! Though the story's
On record, who can handle it? Let's say
Professor Plodd, his mind on inventories,
Amassed an *Atlas of the Milky Way*

—That single galaxy of heaven's zillion—
Giving a page, one page, to every star
(One to our sun and planets), some ten million
Volumes, each tombstone-size, would do. But are
There readers?—even to skim it would, one hears,
At a page a second, take ten thousand years.

The Mouse

This mouse that in my absence haunts the room,
Hunched in a sooty hood, his long palms livid—

When fiercely the lamp surprises him, caught midway
On the great acre of the desk-top, how he
Quivers, a bright-eyed panic with sharp ears.

Now comes the hunter's instinct, to fling books,
To whoop and poke and harass the little trophy.

But, one hand on the light-switch at the door,
I let him have the first move: flat and tightened
He palpitates a moment there, all nerves;
Then, trying to be invisible, nearly succeeding,
He races the cluttered alleys of the desk,
Spins in a rattly junkyard, inches long,

Of paper clips and golf tees, an old key ring.
Skirting the scholar's scribbled pack on cards
Über den ursprünglichen Text des König Lear,
He despairs of reversing his pretty ascent
By trunk of desk-leg or electric liana,
Plops himself clumsy and squeaking to the floor
And under the wall-register scuds in a blur.

All in a moment. My hand leaves the switch;
I cross the room, stare at the desk, discover
What brought him his dark journey three floors up
Through gust and danger of hollow wall: the edge of
My amber artgum nibbled fine, like coinage.

Take it, small earnest ghost.

                         Myself, the giver,
Intrude here in the four walls of dimension,
And probably vex the œconomies of heaven.

JEAN NORDHAUS

Adirondack Return

The faces on the porches
slowly age in their rocking chairs.
Some have aged themselves right down
into the earth and through it,
roots lifting, heaving the stones.

The polestar is not where we left it.
Perhaps it is not the same star. The same
path leads down to the boathouse,
the same rough songs on the jukebox
spill over the lake and dissolve.

The lake itself is zoned
in grays and silvers, gerrymandered
to a map of possibilities, as if we could
retrieve the car, the boys within,
the bar, the lake, the too-bright moon.

Tire-tracks fill with silver, swirling
as we pass. Three hunters leave the lodge
and climb the hill. A truckdoor slams.
A dog raises its head to listen, then
buries it in a bowl. And though we return

to a bend in the road
where things went wrong, here
where waves are always lapping
at the shore, where screen doors slam,
winter is always closing in on trees

and lake and lodge, and nothing
changes this, not even the slow,
spiralling sheaves of rain moving
like witnesses across the mountains,
puckering the lake with bitter warnings.

Protecting the Children from Hurricanes

Nail the shutters closed
and open the faucets,
filling all basins with water.
Make a nest of pillows
and blankets under the stairs,
haul in canned goods

to last for a month—
But whatever you do,
do not warn the children
or imagine you are saving them.
These are your own small rituals,
charms and spells against disaster.

When morning comes, you will scramble eggs
the children will refuse to eat,
clasp a paper which brings no news
against your breast
and leave the cabin
stepping out together into the

lightest air. They will regret
throughout their lives: the long,
sharp teeth of the hemlock trunk
that missed the house, yesterday's
tidy cottages resting on
their roofs, the beach hotel

turned inside out, the jackstraw-timbers
splintered, tumbled guts:
disheveled chairs spilling kapock
like fat women caught without their corsets,
antic tables asleep in the sun, waving
thin legs at the sky.

Bluegrass

We drive to water
Sunday afternoons through second growth,

rivers of bluegrass tumbling from the speaker.
Trees thwang past like banjo strings,
the crickets frail.

Climbing with a camera,
like carrying a child or trying out
a new, vulnerable limb,
we relearn the perils of walking,
cautious over rock.

The trail threads downstream
like a melody, gropes for water,
misses, runs ahead
down blind alleys of rock
toward a promise of green,

plunges back into the woods and
climbs to reach another outcrop.
Along the bank, the juts of rock
lean out and point upstream like cannon
single-sighted, while imagination

edging toward the rim
creeps forward hand by hand, then falters
where the heart drops away like a cliff
to a rope of silt-green river
twisting in the gorge.

Hiking home through spangled woods,
we pass young couples starting out with ropes.
They will lower themselves like grasshoppers
just for sport over the sheerest cliffs,
the ones we couldn't contemplate,

run lightly up and down the strings.

CAROLE SIMMONS OLES

The Cedar Waxwing

What keeps the full weight of my foot
from striking the welcome mat
as I open the door
and stride into morning?
What I so nearly crush belongs
airborne, delivering song
over my third-storey porch rail,
not here, not feathers from peril
where I, just in time, stop.

I try to reconstruct luck—
the failure of screendoor to break
such small bones—or misfortune:
sun at an angle, flight's collision
with window or wall. Perhaps my brute
inattention caused the hurt
I just almost compounded infinitely.
The bird won't move, so I do, bending low
holding my unwieldy breath

to touch the clenched claws, stroke
once the head. Nothing. The black
glass stares. I've never been this close
to a life that ought to rise
from my huge look at its fear.
Crest, black mask, tan-feathered
body, two sparks on a yellow-
dipped tail, paler yellow
under the breast disappearing—

can I rescue such beauty?
Pride and summer make me try.
She's breathing: webs that hang
on branches. To be spare wings,
my fingers close around her.
A hand's evolved to lift a damaged bird
and hold it till whatever.
I feel the voltage under feathers.
I open my palm.

The Radioactive Ball

I caught it
and screamed for water.

Someone carried a pail,
I plunged my hands in.
The water boiled.
I wore violet gloves beaded with glass.

Now what do I do with this water.
How can I pick the pail up,
where should I set it.
How to turn doorknobs and enter rooms
and not lift my child.

Is it too late to cut them off.
Where will I bury them.
If I burn them, who
will breathe the air of their burning.

Throw them into the ozone.
Ship them to Mars,

these death hands.

No pockets will have
them.

GREGORY ORR

Dark Prayer

Long before dawn, anxiety has me
seated on the back porch
staring out to where yesterday
the woods were and now,
in the blackness, nothing is.

Under the noise of first birds
I hear what reassures me:
a muffled clatter and thump
as of scenic flats
being arranged to make
the day's believable landscape—
sounds that indicate
behind the dark curtains
they are hard at work
making the world ex nihilo,
those to whom I pray—
powers invisible, hidden in wings.

The Gray Fox

Someone I know is dying, at seventeen.
When he visited last Thanksgiving
he wore with an adolescent's joy
the black leather jacket I lent him.

Around us spring happens: a crocus
among the gravestones, plum blossoms
that open in a single night.

Already ivy twines the fencewire
and last year's path through the field
is lost in the thick green of new grass.

It would be good to be the gray fox
that trots to pond's edge, spots me
and stops. All winter he's hunted here,
undisturbed, and now he watches me
watch him, ten yards away, unafraid.

The Cliff

Below me, treetops, a crow
making its slow progress.
The green canopy's no sea
or net, but that absolute—
thin veil between
the living and the dead.

Confusion of thickets behind me;
before me, open space.

From time to time returning
to this granite ledge
where I measure my life
by refusals, here
where measuring starts,
less than a step from the edge.

Meadow in Spring

Between the warm wind's
thumb and finger
each bud's rubbed.

And look, indefatigible
saplings
poke through
the soggy tombstone
of a mattress
lovers dragged here
summers ago.

Watchers

> Photographed from the moon, [the Earth] seems
> to be a kind of organism. It's plainly in the
> process of developing, like an enormous
> embryo. It is, for all its stupendous size and the
> numberless units of its life forms, coherent.
> Every tissue is linked for its viability to every
> other tissue.   —Lewis Thomas, The Medusa
> and the Snail

And so I'm linked to you
like cells within a growing embryo,
        and you are linked to me,
and we, together, linked to everyone
        as watchers from the moon can see.

The patient watchers from the moon can tell
        what currents pushing through the tide
direct vast spawnings from the swaying deep,
        and what ancestral pathways
through the buoyant air wedged wild geese keep

        inscribed within their brains
that safely store stupendous images—
        range after range of mountain snow,
        and shadowed woodland green,
blue sky reflected in blue sea below.

        Although they see all parts as one,
wholly dependent and yet numberless,
        the watchers from the moon
surmise some flaw may be developing,
        some rampant cells may soon

outgrow the rest, presuming that their lives
        were all life meant. And yet
        for now, the watchers still are full
        of admiration, awe;
each tissue seems connected, viable—

like you and me, together,
linked as one with our increasing kind,
    taking dominion everywhere,
now cultivating forests, now the seas,
    now blasting even through the air.

    The membrane of the sky
holds in accumulated oxygen,
    welcomes the visible, good light,
protects from lethal ultraviolet,
    and guards against the flight

of random meteors that burn out,
harmless at the edge of our home space, as if
    by miracle, although
just friction from our atmosphere is what
    the watchers from the moon must know

    keeps us alive and linked
each to the other, each to the sunlit cycles
    of exhaling plants and trees.
For pollination, fruits and flowers have
    warm winds and their obliging bees;

forests renew themselves from their decay,
    aided by intermittent rain;
and plankton, drifting in the sun to breed,
    provide the herring and the whale
    with all the food they need

    to keep revolving life alive
        in this appointed place—
to which we're linked and which replenishes
    ambrosia of the air
    and animates the sea that says

    *Coherence is the law
we must obey*, although the watchers see
    certain relentless cells below,
dividing, and divided from the rest,
    forming a monster embryo.

It Would Have Been Enough

If only daffodils had caught the light,
           that would have been enough;
      and if to add variety,
           just crocuses and tulips
      splashed their colors in the dawn,
           that, too, would have sufficed;
      and if just sparrows, common sparrows,
not white-throated, dusky-evening, golden-crowned,
      had tilted on a limber bough
amid the silver smooth and silver rough
      and twined their whistlings in the leaves,
           that would have been enough.
To add variety, it would have been enough
           if only chickadees,
      the plain gray junco, and the nuthatch
also frequented the maple tree and played
           upon a puff of wind,
and, certainly, it would have been sufficient
      if, beside the steady maple,
for the sake of contrast in the hazy rain,
      a clump of gleaming birches swayed.
It would have been sufficient for variety
           without the tamaracks,
      without the pines, without the firs,
without the hemlocks harboring the wind;
           it would have been enough
to have the chipmunk pausing on his log
           without the browsing deer
who, one by one by one, their white tails flashing,
      leap across the minnow stream.
           We didn't need that much
      to want to make ourselves at home
           and building our dwellings here—
just light upon the lake would have sufficed to see,
           just changing light at evening
on a birch clump or a single maple tree.
      For us to make ourselves at home,
           it would have been enough
if only we had said, "This is enough,"
           and for variety,

it would have been sufficient if we said
　　　　　"This surely will suffice,"
and when dawn brushed its shadows in the apple tree,
　　　　　if we had only said
how bountiful those shaded circles are,
　　　　　how silently they pull
　　　　themselves together toward the stem,
that bounty would have seemed more bountiful.
　　　　　And even now, if I should say,
"How bountiful," then just one daffodil,
　　　　　a single daffodil unfolding
　　　　　in a yellow vase
upon a maple table in the breeding sun,
　　　　　would be enough
　　　　and seem abundant far beyond
what was sufficient to desire, except
　　　　　for one brown, ordinary sparrow
　　　　　on my windowsill,
which I cannot resist including in this light,
　　　　and maybe one wide row of cedars,
winding up the valley to the misted hill.

Bounty

> *Incredible elaborations of the flowering plants*
> *kept exploding. The angiosperms had taken over*
> *the world. Grass was beginning to cover the*
> *bare earth, and all kinds of vines and bushes*
> *squirmed and writhed under new trees with*
> *flying seeds. . . . Apes [evolved into]men*
> *because flowers had produced seeds and fruits*
> *in such tremendous quantities that a new and*
> *totally different store of energy had become*
> *available.*
> 　　—Loren Eisley, The Immense Journey

　　Here come exploding waves
of wind-borne ovaries with seeds inside,
　　　　each like a little astronaut—
angiosperms are landing everywhere,
　　　　they've taken hold, having been taught

by parent genes to hunker down, dig in,
　　　　grasp hard and cling with fibrous roots.

Incredible elaborations now appear
            by rivers and by lakes,
in forests, deserts, plains—they settle here

            with power to proliferate,
creeping or swaying, climbing, reaching out;
            each in its own determined way
            appropriates a space
in which to greet the light, where it can stay.

            The mustard family,
the family of peas, of carrot, and of mint,
            the aster-daisy family,
stretch out as squirming vine or writhing bush;
            extending even to the sea,

they cover every barren inch of earth.
            The grasses, ah, the grasses,
thousands of rough, colonizing variants
            are replicating what they are—
            as if the only sense

under the photosynthesizing sun
            is to renew yourself
a million fold into a universe of seeds
            that flowers always into *you*,
            a universe that breeds,

            yes, *you*, again and yet again
with no end but your own prodigious self,
            unchanged, becoming more,
still more, of what precisely you have been.
            But now a totally new store

            of vital energy,
a grazer's plenitude, transforms how eating
            fares upon the fertile earth.
Plants must make way for ungulates, and thus
            devourers flourish at the birth

            of still another era
as the world becomes a cornucopia—
            a romping goat god's gift to please

the dazed apes gaping at
such quantities of fruit upon the trees

it seems provided just for them.
For them the bushes flower
and the shrubs, the vines, the pungent herbs;
for them red berries ripen as exploding
bounty of the earth disturbs

their sweetened lips to shape
their needed words, "All mine, all this is mine!"
until an echo from the sky
rolls out as a resounding, absolute command:
Be fruitful, multiply,

replenish all the earth, subdue the beasts,
and take dominion over
every living thing! becomes their holy text,
though some hunched fear within their seed
dreads what elaborations will seize power next.

Fathering the Map

In May of nineteen-hundred forty-two,
my father's birthday gift to me
was a long, cardboard map,
extending from green England in the west,
past purple Germany,
beige Russia, east to red Japan.
We hung it in the basement playroom where
I tended my aquariums
of turtles, salamanders, frogs, and kept
my pen of flop-eared rabbits,
my wood hutch of guinea pigs who slept
within my tended peace.
My father's plan was that together
we would track the progress of the war.
He bought a box of colored pins
to represent each country's tanks and troops
so that we could "keep score"
of Allied victories, but I recall

the black pins spreading out
across two darkened continents.
By August, cricket calls contending in the night,
my father's faulty health turned bad
as German armies camped
beside the Volga river outside Stalingrad,
and it occurred to me
for the first time that we might lose—
that purposes beyond
my comprehension might have chosen us
to know defeat: we Jews,
even here in America,
would be exterminated when the Nazis came.
In nineteen forty-five,
we moved because my father died: two strokes
had left him speechless,
though his eyes were still alive
when I last sat with him.
I had to give my turtles to the zoo,
my salamanders and my frogs,
my flop-eared rabbits and my guinea pigs,
and every loss I knew
went with them as if loss could be restored
in a protected place.
The day the moving truck arrived,
I cleared our cluttered map, pin by cold pin,
from yellow Naples up to Finland,
orange Normandy to rainbow-hued Berlin,
but left it on the basement wall
in case the kid who came
to live there in my house could find
some other use for it, some other game.
But that was forty years ago.
I never met the boy
who moved in after me, and I don't know
what he did with our map—
perhaps his father threw it out, replaced
it on the wall when we sent troops
to South Korea, or they might have traced
the torrid Gaza wars
so they could bear and understand
the unchanged passions of
the shifting borders of the holy Land.

Maybe the boy who moved in next
received a birthday map of the whole world—
        as if his father were to say:
                keep count of oil spills
        and each rain forest, stripped of trees,
whose species we exterminate each day;
        remember the first covenant
                Jehovah made with Noah
following the flood: *Neither shall flesh*
        be cut off to destroy the earth.
                Maybe his father's eyes
        were fresh with tears as if he meant
                to keep a vow: "Mute death
is unredeemable; I can't accept
        our breaking of the covenant."
                The map I'll leave my son
will look like moonlight seething on the sea—
        all blank but for a single pin
                to represent an ark,
in hope another covenant to save the earth
                may find words in the dark.

Mountain Ash without Cedar Waxwings

The likely last nostalgic warmth of autumn
                has gone by, the amber leaves
have fallen from the mountain ash, and still
                luminescent berries
        hold their positions on the chill,
stiff branches, clustered together like orange stars,
        because no cedar waxwing's come
                to stuff its horny mouth
                in preparation for
        its migratory journey south.
Listen! for I'm no longer sure I know
        what words can reach the words in you,
                though words have been my life,
no cedar waxwing's visited my tree
                four bleak falls in a row,
after a quarter of a century
                according to my watch,

because their southern habitat
has been deforested at the dumbfounding rate
of eighty-two square miles a day.
And watching their not dwelling here a while,
watching the silent way
the orange berries seem to cry out
for the yellow blur of flurried wings
that gives the gaudy gold
of autumn its autumnal burnishing,
summons to memory
the losses I could not have known
life on this planet would inflict on me.
I knew I'd have to face my aging
and my death, but not
the death of forests, not of oceans, not the air;
I knew I'd lose my parents,
lose unsuspecting friends,
but not the mournful bond that lets us share
consoling voices from the past,
not faith in our true mother tongue that seemed,
hardly a rhyme ago,
generative as April mist,
evocative as February snow.
But now, dishonored and demeaned,
language itself, like ravaged earth, betrays
its own betrayers who
betray the laughter Chaucer knew,
betray Shakespearean remorse, whose mind,
beyond all anger and all tears,
as breeding as the sun,
could empathize with everyone.
These are not losses of my own,
losses that I can bear,
my temporary life,
but loss of what I once thought permanent—
the woods, the oceans, and the air,
loss of the binding words
that mean the meanings their intenders meant.
Is it too late for me to say,
for better or for worse,
I feel as empty as my mountain ash
without the cedar waxwings here,
I feel the loss, wide as our universe,
of everything that I hold dear?

JAY PARINI

Mizzle

The sodden weather of an early spring:
loose gravel on the road, the ice-floes melting
in the brook behind a patch of hemlocks.

I could smell the pine-tar, mud and mint,
the stink of fox: a wan slow smell
in winds that gathered from a nearby swamp.

The deadly owl's asleep by rosy dawn,
but one fat raven lifts its wings
and veers into a field and drops from sight.

They say that somewhere in this range of hills
a man still wanders who left home last year,
an old man looking for the end of time.

A thousand stumps that stud the swampland
once were something you might want to climb;
I watch them sink to silt and crumble,

decomposing in the same sure way
that everything we love at last undoes
its laces, sighs at ease, then lays

its head down, nuzzles into loam,
relinquishing the lovely stand of life
to meld, the slow atomic mince and slaughter.

Some Compensation

Trees in the forest fall and, falling, find
some compensation in the way they fail.
The mites become them, riddling the bark
that loosens slowly over many summers
as the fog surrounds and seeps inside.

A punky softness is the telltale sign
that what was once so thoroughly contained
in lines of strict and vertical composure
has begun to let itself begin
as earth and water, air and maybe fire:
combustible, a decomposing mass
where energy converts itself again
from this to that, shape-shifting spirit—
protean and pure in each new guise.
So pocks are filled with exoskeletons
and digging legs, with flywings, dust of eggs
that hatch and swarm; a nest is broken
and becomes a teeming, homely city
where a worm may sleep and fall to slush;
where what was wood is turned to gases
that will heal the sky; where tubers feed,
the tiny shoots emerging, gaining into green,
absorbing water that has been contained
in spongy pulp, in moss that covers
with assuaging fur the log's bare skin.
What a feast is made of what has fallen,
and the wind, as patient now as ever,
circles and assumes this shape or that one,
always moving on: from leaf to lizard,
seed to finch to splatter in the mud,
where breath begins, where eyes fall open,
where the world invents itself again.

Bliss

It's happening: the full fell fall,
a coverlet of days that loop around
my shoulders as my feet sink low
in mulch or mud, the quintessential *drech*
betokening another loss of summer, light and love.
I was taught to sag, to wear
this garment of adieu with circumspection
and address the past—*O fair have fallen*!
Dank, dark, dunk: I sop along the path,
a somber trace through leaf-burnt umber,
and address my sorrows, line by line,
a threadbare cloak or quilt or whatnot,

text or textures I have worn before.
But somehow I'd prefer a finer truth:
I'd like this fall, its fatal slippage, decomposing
what I took for granted once too often—
darkened woods, a lost position
on the middle way from here to there.
I'd like to hide among the drips, the withering
of trees, the bird-abandoned blaze of branches
that will soon be bone-fire, blackened limbs,
bereft and crumbling but at peace, my home
amid the grainy sands of snow and gravel,
the unending bliss of nothing more.

Belonging

I do not belong here
in a summer field at midnight, walking.

It is not my world, however much
I love the brightness falling from the air,
the slur of tires on blackened roads,
freesia in the wind,
the long wet grass around my knees.

A million crickets work their wings:
they multiply, divide, play all the numbers
and survive in noisy August clouds.
One anthill underfoot is Nineveh or Rome,
depending on how close I care to look.
An owl is steady in the highborn oak
and watching for what moves.
A green eye tilts beneath a log.

In China,
one old man is sitting by a yew;
he's puzzling over what he never said
to one who died.
In hot Zimbabwe, there is someone's mother
by the bloody ditch
without a word of explanation.
In Salvador, a small girl asks for more.

So many stories.
I would hear them all.
Write down each sentence till the pages tore,
till ink was spittle
and the world's last tear returned to ocean
and my flesh was dirt.

Tonight, however, I will speak
but for myself.

The sky snows stars.
I feel the slow, compulsive spinning
of the globe through night,
the axle of the earth
that drives a needle through my heart again.
I hear the high and spectral whine
of unborn spirits wanting more.
I won't pretend to welcome,
wave them down.

It's not my world to give away.

Stars Falling

Fire-flakes, flints: the same old stars
still fiery in the unredemptive sky,
the silvery and hopeless midnight sky
that feels like home from here to Mars,
then gradually grows foreign into stars
we hardly recognize, that fill the eye
with lofty gleanings we ineptly scry
by framing legends of unending wars.

There is some comfort in the way they sprawl,
their vast composure in the cold and careless
spaces that absorb them as they fall,
their dwindling into dark with less and less
of anything a witness might recall,
the ease of their becoming homelessness.

LINDA PASTAN

The Birds

are heading south, pulled
by a compass in the genes.
They are not fooled
by this odd November summer,
though we stand in our doorways
wearing cotton dresses.
We are watching them

as they swoop and gather—
the shadow of wings
falls over the heart.
When they rustle among
the empty branches, the trees
must think their lost leaves
have come back.

The birds are heading south;
instinct is the oldest story.
They fly over their doubles,
the mute weathervanes,
teaching all of us
with their tailfeathers
the true north.

Hardwood

Do these gnarled and twisted trees
feel greenness surge
at their roots the way saplings do?
When a new leaf breaks through
are they astonished,
as Sarah must have been,
at such an improbable birth?

The woodpecker, with its
firing squad rat-tat-tat, knows
each vulnerable spot on the wrinkled bark.
In a month these trees will resurrect
a shade to sit beneath.
There are stumps
to rest on everywhere.

Beall Mountain Seasonal

1. Columbus Day

Tentative
as envoys to
an undiscovered
country,
the first leaves
come circling down on
the sweet currents
of Indian summer
air, each leaf
its own
small vessel,
a dozen
colored sails
becoming
an armada.
And soon
the world we know
will disappear
behind us,
and what will be
discovered
is simply
winter.

2. Thanksgiving

like a secret
suddenly disclosed

a deer at the window
fills the morning

with the silence
of grace, mouth

full of delicate
leaves,

and in one blink
straightens its arced back

into a disappearing
arrow

     3. The First Day of Winter

How many birds
will disappear
today, taking
their songs with them,

leaving behind
not silence
but the rasping sound
of the wind

honing
its razored edge
along the branches
of trees

the color
of all the autumns
rusted away
already.

ROBERT PINSKY

The City Dark

In the early winter dusk the broken city dark
Seeps from the tunnels. Up towers and in gusty alleys,

The mathematical veil of generation has lit its torches
To light the rooms of the mated and unmated: the two

Fated behind you and four behind them in the matrix
Widening into the past, eight, sixteen, thirty-two,

Many as the crystal dream cells illuminating the city.
Even for those who sleep in the street there are lights.

Like a heavy winter sleep the long flint cold of the past
Spreads over the glinting dream-blisters of the city, asleep

Or awake, as if the streets were an image of the channels
Of time, with sixty-four, one hundred and twenty-eight,

The ancestral net of thousands only a couple of centuries back,
With its migrations and fortunes and hungers like an image

Of the city where the star-dispelling lights have climbed
And multiplied over the tenements and outlying suburbs

Like a far past of multitudes behind us in the glistering web
Of strands crossing, thousands and tens of thousands

Of lives coupled with their gains, passions, misfortunes.
Somewhere in the tangled alleyways, a rape. Somewhere

A spirit diffused winglike, blind along the stretched wires
Branching the dark city air or bundled under the streets,

Coursing surely to some one face like an ancient song *Do re*,
Re la sol sol. Somewhere misfortune, somewhere recognition.

Back here one died of starvation, here one thrived. Descendant,
The bitter city work and the shimmering maternal burden

Of music uncoil outward on the avenues through smokey bars,
By televisions, beyond sleepers while the oblivion of generation

Radiates backward and then forward homeward to the one voice
Or face like an underground pool, through its delicate lightshaft

Moonlit, a cistern of light, echoing in a chamber cellared under
The dark of the city pavement, the faintly glittering slabs.

In Berkeley

Afternoon light like pollen.

This is my language, not the one I learned.

We hungry generations with our question
Of shapes and changes, *Did you think we wanted
To be like you?*

I flicker and for a second
I'm picking through rubbish
To salvage your half-eaten muffin, one hand
At my ear to finger a rill of scab.

Not native
To California, with olive and silver
Leaves like dusty sickles flashing
In the wind, the eucalyptus bend
And whisper it to the hillsides, Did you think
We wanted to be like you?
The tall flourishers, not what they were.

I sniff one and lift my leg and leave
A signature of piss.

Or the feathery stalks of fennel
Burgeoning in the fissured pavement crazed
And canted by the Hayward Fault.

Outside the mosque or commune they grow chin-high,
Ghostly, smelling of anise
In the profligate sun—
Volunteers, escapees, not what they were.

A tile-domed minaret clad in cedar shingle
Grafted at a corner of the shingle house.
A Sufi mother and child come out, the boy
In mufti, shuffling his sneakers through the duff,
Holding her hand.

Mother.

Her cotton tunic and leggings are white,
And from the tapering pleated cylinder
Of her white vertical headdress
To the shoes white like nurse's shoes
Except for her hands and pink face
She is a graceful series of white tubes
Like an animated sheet. I wonder if
They shave their heads. Did you think we
Wanted to be like you?

Sister. Once maybe a Debbie or June,
A Jewish sophomore
From Sacramento or a cornsilk daughter
From Fresno or Modesto.

She puts me in the carseat, she fastens my belt.

Conversion. The shaven, the shriven, the circumcised,
The circumscribed—her great-grandmother
Bleeding a chicken, in her matron's wig
Not what she was.
And Malcolm's brother
Telling him in visiting hours *Don't eat pork*
So that he sat down Saul, and got up Paul.

The demonstrator
At the Campanile in her passion
Shouting at a white haired professor
As he passed, *Old man—why don't you die?*

Forgive me little mother that I will savor
The flesh of pigs. We have forgotten
The Torah and the Koran, on every
Work day and holy day alike
We take up harvesting knives and we sweat
Gathering the herbs of transformation. This
Is my language, not the one I learned.

"Everywhere I Go, There I Am"

Hot days of errands and badges, paper, shrill rage
Of sparrows morning and evening. At sunset
A clearing stroll around the square and down
A steep street twisting to the edge of the narrows,

The brick embankment path and the iron rail
The same as always. The water. All through your body
A steady twinkling of ceasing and being, the cells
That die by millions and replicate themselves

So every seven years your substance is new,
But the same score, the same scar making a faint
Crescent along your temple, always fading,
The blood all different but the same from day

To day, the city birds along the harbor
Working the cracks and hedges, the titan moan
Of a tanker blasting and receding, the range
Of noises a fretwork of the bay, the night.

Dove

Shapes as a series of edges, each edge
a wave exhausted yet extended just
enough until the shoulder is complete,
or the leaf or the chair, which is flying,
which, if we weren't flying too, we could see—
it is a beautiful shoulder, either
elegant or useful, like a calla
lily or cello or a mountain road,
it is a big, flat-handed, star-point oak,
and a rocker, elder, utterly still.
Shapes as the sunlight serial in light,
the sadness of the blur in the picture,
bend of the wing, the white wing-bars, white
edges that at any distance become
integral to the losses of objects
wasting into the air like grain above
the harvest, like the close-up once I saw
of the type hitting the paper like a
hammer, exploding on the high desert
proving-ground of the page in such a way
that dust along the outline of the ink
rose in a shadow of fine dead powder.
The way touching would be fingerprinted
if the flesh could somehow hold the fracture.
Waves of heat, waves of the river rising
from the river, the rainbow edges like
those lines in earth drawn with sticks that will be
straight but not in this life, love, nor money.

In Answer to Amy's Question What's a Pickerel

Pickerel have infinite, small bones, and skins
of glass and black ground glass, and though small for pike
are no less wall-eyed and their eyes like bone.

Are fierce for their size, and when they flare
at the surface resemble drowning birds,
the wing-slick panic of birds, but in those
seconds out of water on the line,
when their color changes and they choose for life,
will try to cut you and take part of your hand
back with them. And yet they open like hands,
the sweet white meat more delicate in oil,
to be eaten off the fire when the sun
is level with the lake, the wind calm,
the air ice-blue, blue-black, and flecked with rain.

Dusk Coming on outside _____, New York

A kind of mountain pond or lake,
the kind of algae-stillness sudden wind kicks up,
the way the spring wind out of Canada is scooping up the surface,
forcing the swans to ride in harness,
all pointed in the same direction,
dozens of them, lucent, whiter in the rain,
some of them feeding, some at attention—

a kind of gravity water tilted on a line toward where the sun
would be, the ghost-dance of the sun,
the pale green clouds of the hillsides lifting,
blurring on the windshield's mica-points of light,
miles of the storm's bright scalloping
bending into wavelengths through the glass
with the fluency of water, water's cold gray eyes.

Human Excrement

   The detail and distinguishing odor,
the sight of it in nature, the odd
   fragment on the sidewalk or at the edge
along the skeletal shrub, where those who
   look down or feel small in the world see the
new order like a trail of pins or mother-
   of-pearl, the starling picked apart like eyes.

Whoever it was had to squat down hard
in the dark and hold breath like a diver,
    had to shut out the lights of the cars and noise,
as the failed intimacy of the body
    was once more counted against us, so human
after all, so animal or angry,
    this answer to longing and our hunger.

The Offset

Some miles beyond the last reef's barricade,
Where currents take the local tide to sea
And where, long from the seaward looking cottage,
The gulls tease, hover, and descend, as lightly
As a maple's keys coptering and lost
Over the general waters off this coast,
There the charts agree what's out of range . . .
And there, the practical keel that can't divide
What it crosses divides its way anyway,
Cutting one course from all others, tossed
But steady on the contoured gray.

Just so, because there's any course to take
But only one that's taken right,
And even when it's right then only true
By going off a bit, crabbing its way . . .
As all good pilots learn to do,
Sighting a line that's never without play
And traveling the way the light things go,
Not ahead but spindrift and sideways of sight,
As the imagination does sometimes
To get things right, though seeming to know,
Really off course a bit, but more promising so.

Haying

They are gathering hay. The truck rolls slowly.
The men walk on either side, lifting bales,
Talking without looking up. When one truck fills
Another takes its place, the loaded truck
Turning for the barn, where another crew waits
To get the bales up to the loft.
                                There is a boy
They've hired for one day; he gets half wages.
They've put him at the top where it's hot,

Where he drags the bales from the lazy belt.
He can't lift the bales, so he backs then tugs,
Backs then tugs, feeling the barn's tin roof bake down.

They've worked since 6 a.m. and now the sun
Enlarges through the trees, which line the field's
Far edge, where the other crew follows a truck.
The older men wear overalls; the young men
Are stripped to the waist. The boy still wears his shirt.
Twice he has tried tobacco, twice gotten sick,
But now he is tired and elated,
Seeing the field's last load turning towards the barn.

Then tugging a bale, he brushes the nest.
And there are yellow jackets everywhere.
And the stings are everywhere, under his shirt,
On his ears, down each arm, and he is running,
Tripping, stung, running again, stung, climbing
Through the stings and rolling along the loft,
Another sting, and the loft's floor opening

And he sees the battered truck, the men circled
And he is on the truck's bed looking up,
The men still circled, and gazing down.
They don't move him, they will not move him,
And he can't move himself.
                         Old Smythe bends near
And puts tobacco on the stings.
He breaks a cigarette, chews the tobacco,
Then puts it on a sting—here, there, another . . .
Then another cigarette.
                         He asks the boy
Can he move his legs. The boy says, no,
Yes, maybe . . . maybe in a minute.

The men talk on, as calmly as before—
Complain about the heat, swat flies, light up.
The doctor's on his way and it's alright
Because they meant to quit, needed to,
Else they would have started the next field
And never gotten home.
                         Lie there, boy,
And listen to their neutral voices—

Used for selecting seed, planting, calving,
Used when ringing necks or cutting calves to steers,
Used for harvest, slaughter, funerals, drought—
And August always turns to drought,
One baking gust that cures the grass
Like a breath inhaled and held
So long that light turns colors.

The Elbow Tree

A sapling bent and tied to point the way,
First it looked deformed, then got another form,
From getting read by the tribes who followed it.
The insistent elbow, locked and freakish looking,
Could make a match for any highway sign
Except each year the elbow stretched a bit,
Until in time the posture grew extreme,
With limbs pointing upward to one side,
And the tree still signing silently,
"This way, and you will not be lost."

Thus understood, no exaggeration changed
What the tree became, nothing altered
What the living figure grew to mean
To those who knew the way and bent the tree
And those who read the figure and followed,
While the trunk and limbs increased with age,
Knotting in potency above the seeds
That fell countless and unaccountable
In blinding freedom from the tree that was
In one thing deprived and in another made.

For Barbara, Who Brings a Green Stone in the Shape of a Triangle

From ocean
this porous shape
indisputably green
color I tell you
of healing, the color
I have chosen around me
like a vapor, this towel
on my shoulders, its green
drape an air over my scar,
then a shirt I pull over my head
and let fall for the green
lint-shed filaments of healing, moss
some ancestor might bind up with spit
and press onto my breast, no, the space
where my breast has been.
       Yesterday
for the space of an hour, a woman
came here with her child, raised
up shirt, her breast was flesh.
The child pulled where her nipple
is, and touched his mouth
to her and filled himself.
She talked as he drank.
I listened to nipple,
a hiss of milk.
Miracle.

In your photos of green ocean
and boats, a line of women in green air,
their arms muscular, pulls against green water.
Their breasts are bare.
One, yours, shows a faint scar
my skin wears.
      In the past year
I have given up four of the five organs

the body holds to call itself woman.
                                        Green
healer, today my body carries
in its clever hand the triangle
sea gave up to you
and you gave me.

                                I press it to my chest,
empty of nipple, of milk, of nurture,
and feel you there: friend, lover
of women, teacher. You speak to me
each green vowel of the life language.

Teaching, Hurt

Bradshaw, Nebraska near York, forty-eight miles
the spring of the heart
loud under its breast, wild heart at its single lesson,
spring of sterile apples, trees a pyramid of white
spectacle overflowing buttermilk at twilight,
spring of buttermilk, shorter life, the body's affairs
heart broken under its absent breast the beat so loud
she fancies they can hear it thud
in a room loud with her perfume's diversion.

Spring teaching again, early morning gone to the highway by six
single, alone, fields ripening in some color
she can't anymore name. Bradshaw, Bradshaw,
rhymes with bedsore, rhymes with bad law, rhymes with
lockjaw, the first day she can't find a place
to work without disturbing someone.
At lunch the teacher names her boys
twins, and an older. "It could be worse," she laughs
out loud, delighted, and someone whispers yes,
the first child has cancer in his brain.

Into this mess, new life:
week-old Peking ducks, and mallards, grey brown
and plain, some with green heads
you can't tell yet which is which, girl from boy;
a Hamburg chick, sole survivor of the trip from Omaha,

flat comb, wide tail feathers, an exotic;
and Partridge Cochin, feathers down to their golden feet,
colored like pheasants; twelve babies in a Wheat Chex box
small as first graders who make the circle work
holding chicks onto their newspapers. The water dish
overflows onto the floor of the lunchroom where the kids
make nests of their legs to sit watching
and she hunches over them, hungry to see
what they see, to see them.

IRA SADOFF

In the Bog behind My House

The crows have come back for April
and the first buds, the hyacinths.
They leave winter for the hearty chickadees.

They love the muddy ditches
dressed with possums, mice, and skunks.
Crows find the mist inviting, the fog banks

where deer have been slumbering—wounded deer
who limped through winter. We could say
crows are cynical, shadows on the wall, our wings

flapping, our jaws chewing with a sudden fury.
We could say the sound of crows is a chasm.
The way I see the bog behind my house

it is always April. It is always April
when I feel the sheen of black and blue.
When I hear them picking clean the sparrow wings.

God, teach me how to love the crows
for being crows, to care for those
the crows won't spare, without becoming them.

I Join the Sparrows

I join the sparrows
in the snow. As one of them,
I stir the kingdom up
and to their busy fluttering
add a chirp. If I could
make a sound to satisfy
the heavens, like wind
through paper, a harp

of wings, if I could join
the kingdom of the startled
constantly, I'd lose my
worldly wife, the snow-capped
mountain view, the death I earned
by laboring. God, speak to me
through sparrows, insist
we're not waste and water.
The sunlight fading
late December holds no lesson
for the living. Perched
on earthly wings, above
the bog where sparrows mate
and make their home,
I sing awhile, a high, faint trill.

Red Tail Sonnet

"No more soaring," said the hawk with a gunshot wound.
"I'd trade in these wings for a few sizzling sunsets."
From this height the hawk looks regrettable, fretful,
an L-shaped shrug. Untouchable, that's immortality
for those who feel the slug in their chests, watching him.
When we view the dead animal, its calls up the species
soaring above us, giving us pause. Its red tail a pale apple,
a mouse in its claws, a wriggling snake its signature.
Hours I watched him, above the highway line, waiting
and diving, the draft of air seizing him at his peak.
I wanted him to sit on my shoulder and screech. But
emblems are for the living, for those who learn to change.
We project misery best. The hawk, with flies
all around it, the pearl of his beak pursed to speak.

On the Job

I support the animals' urge to survive.
So much for opinions. Slithering, writhing,
nosing my way through dirt, I can identify

with that. I joke to keep the system going.
So whatever the effect of clearing island fog
with concomitant deer nibbling berry bushes

at dusk, I keep my distance. I keep the home office
—pencil scratches, accommodating memos, bows—
yawning. But the gnawing animal stalks us,

keeps us feeding and feeling weak. Garcia Lorca
once said, "When the moon rises, the heart feels
like an island in infinity." Who can improve on that?

My labor must mean something. The worn salt lick,
narrow paths and droppings in my meadow, velvet residue
of antlers, all are real enough. I keep the hunters out.

Birches, Revisited: October

At last the silver birches look like Frost,
archaic as he must have seen them
in Vermont. My nostalgia's not for him,
but for the alders, priests who skim
the granite on our hill at any cost,
passing judgments on the ridge, the hem
of malls and sturdy parking lots
I cringe past and use. Tainted emblems of our lust
for sultry trinkets. Bodies pay their fees
for breathing, and all our tortured writhing
soothes us on our way to heaven.
Spirits suffer anyway, each fall.
Sentimental trees—spindly, cold and tall—
birches stand in spite of us and poetry
that praises "nature" like a long lost friend,
we who drive for groceries, shoes, and pens.

SHEROD SANTOS

The Dairy Cows of Maria Cristina Cortes

Although they may be
the most mothering of all the animals,
the ones with the gentlest
complaint, the ones whose milk
has left on our tongues
the knowledge that life can be simple
and good, still,

in their pendulous,
earth bound, solitary ways, they remind me
of nothing quite so much
as those people we become after
the houselights rise
on a movie that finds us wiping back
a tear. And since

sadness, however
privately borne, secreted however far inside,
is a thing that finally
weighs us down, they are also
the ones most likely
in the end to inherit the earth; so wherever
they go, wandering

the mud lanes out
from the dairy, or wading into grasses
at a pond's edge, they
move the way a slow-forming storm
cloud moves, gathering
within it a heaviness drawn from deep
in the soil,

a heaviness it will
return there. And yet a cow jumped over
the moon, we're told, and
what in the world has ever been

more filled with light
than a glass of milk placed by the bed
of a child still struggling

from a nightmare?
But whatever it is we say about the cow,
it's the face we love,
a face that in spite of what we do
with our fences and barbs
and electrically charged cattle prods
shines equally on us

as on the grasses
of the world; and shines in a way that makes
us feel forgiven after all
for forgetting we, too, are animals—base-
born, landlocked, spattered
with mud, and filled with an ancient cow-
sorrow and -wonder.

Of Haloes & Saintly Aspects

Out of a ripple in the sea grass,
Two unhoused fiddler crabs
Sidestep past the almost-dead

Hawksbill turtle turned over
On the beach and left there
Staked with a length of broom-

Stick and baling wire. The squared,
Inquiring head upstraining,
The plastron split, and the sun-

Dazed eyes that will not weep
For such incongruities as these:
Faced into the current of an on-

Shore breeze, the once-buoyant
Cradle of its shell closes like
A trench around its breathing.

Now anchored to the earth,
It founders in the slipstream
Of a mild, inverted sea, and

Labors toward it still, its little
Destiny undisturbed by acts
Of forgiveness or contrition.

Still Life with Minnows

The river, while it
runs the gamut of all idle
eyes gathered on the sandbar,
whirlpools in around a snagged
tree-limb trailing the red
flag of the drowned

girl's blouse, though
her body was hauled out
hours ago. Just moments before
that moment, she'd wrestled with
her brothers while her father
spilled a dipnet full

of minnows in a
mason jar, and now the jar,
the net, the flattened reeds beside
their fishing poles, remain as they
could not help but remain;
now, in an upstairs

bedroom five farms
down the road, the oldest
brother sets his teeth into his thumb
and sees it just that way, the min-
nows still blindly bump-
ing at the glass.

Augury

Your pinking, winter-white shoulders bent
Over the flower bed's rubble, soggy

Still from the snow-melt this week loaded
Underground, at body heat, in April.

I'd stayed inside, although behind my upstairs
Window I wasn't really imagining things

When I watched a field rat bore back out
From the woodpile tumbled behind you; or when,

Sinking my pitchfork into the collapsed
Mulch-pile, a blacksnake speared by the tines

Wound up like a caduceus along the handle.
Nevertheless, there you were, made over again

By my own deliberate confusions: bare-
Shouldered, burning, imperilled in the yard.

Sawdust

They've cut down the old sugar maple
that stood for more than one hundred years
on our lawn in a line with her five other sisters
since at least my Great-grandmother was born.
Late October, the leaves lay in rusting heaps
under a sky raw with storm.

The tree *looked* ill.
All summer it ailed, its trunk
filigreed with lichen.
Last year's drought, and years of acid rain—
the hundred gallons of fertilizer
we pumped into the ground around its roots
was like water down a drain.
We got a second opinion.
The next big storm, if a big branch fell,
we were responsible.

Late morning, the truck arrived
with heavy equipment,
and two men and a crane.
After filling their chain-saws with gasoline,
one man climbed into the elevator bucket
which levitated him high into the branches.
To the hard-hatted men who look like surfers,
trees are a religion.

They switched on their saws
and began the chain-saw mating call,
the deafening whines
pushing higher and higher in tandem.
The man in the tree lashed himself, like Odysseus
to the mast, to his bucket in the branches,
while the other shouted,
supervising from the ground.

There is a strategy
for cutting down a tree.
You start from the bottom up,
making your selection,
then work your way up the trunk,
roping the main branches,
lopping off a branch, a larger branch.
The dead ones hit the ground with a hollow sound.

High in the second story bedroom,
my breath fogged the window.
Sawdust sprinkling the grass like snow.

Then the tree stood, a naked torso.
A deep V cut into the trunk, down low.

Then the tree fell.

No need to get sentimental.

After they cut the trunk into logs and raked the lawn
and stacked the kindling,
and fed the twigs and branches to the grinder
that chewed them into chips,

it was quiet,
quieter than before,
quieter than the world was, ever.

Old tree, Great-grandmother,
your stump staring straight up into the sky.

For the first time we had
a clear view of the road,

the rising moon.
A consolation.

And for the next two days,
our elderly neighbor, Morris,
split logs that would last him the winter;
his ax, a heartbeat shaking our house.

ROBERT SIEGEL

Slug

White, moist, orange,
I crawl up the cabbage leaf exposed,
too much like your most intimate parts
to be lovely, to be loved. I weep
to the world, my trail a long tear,
defenseless from its beaks and claws
except for my bitter aftertaste.
He who touches me shares my sorrow
and shudders to the innermost—my pale horns
reaching helpless into the future.
In plastic cups filled with beer
ringed like fortresses around your garden,
your lie of plenty,
we drown by the hundreds,
curled rigid in those amber depths,
so many parentheses surrounding nothing.
You do not understand nothing:
the nakedness to the sky,
the lack of one protective shelter,
the constant journey.
Millions of us wither in the margins
while food rots close by.
Nothing is a light that surrounds us
like the breath of God.

Turtles

They have thought upon this log
since before Socrates
climbed into the light,
or Plato

settled for silence,
or Aristotle

brought out his bottles
and labels.

Each crawls up on a deadhead
with the other philosophers.
Dull as old coins, old helmets,
they do not speak,

but there are subtle
inflections of the throat,
and eyes, half-lidded,
which stare at a question,

and a mouth that holds onto
a conclusion.
Each day adds to their library
a reflection of twigs,

a silver razzle of minnows,
or a new shade of green.
Though their council is old,
no one has spoken.

Sunlight like moss
heavy on his tongue,
their chairman is still
clearing his throat.

Silverfish

It lives in the damps of rejection,
    in the dark drain, feeding upon the effluvia
        of what we are, of what we've already been.

Everything comes down to this: we are its living—
    the fallen hair, the fingernail, the grease from a pore,
        used toothpaste, a detritus of whiskers and dead skin.

All this comes down and worries it into life,
    its body soft as lymph, a living expectoration,
        a glorified rheum. In the silent morning

when we least expect it, it is there
    on the gleaming white porcelain: the silver scales,
        the many feelers *busy busy*, so fast, it is

unnerving, causing a certain panic in us,
    a galvanic revulsion (*Will it reach us
        before we reach it?*), its body

translucent, indefinable, an electric jelly
    moving with beautiful sweeps of the feet
        like a sinuous trireme, delicate and indecent,

sexual and cleopatric. It moves for a moment
    in the light, while its silver flashes and slides,
        and part of us notices an elusive beauty,

an ingenious grace in what has been cast off.
    As if tears and the invisibly falling dandruff,
        skin cells and eyelashes

returned with an alien and silken intelligence,
    as if chaos were always disintegrating into order,
        elastic and surprising,

as if every cell had a second chance
    to link and glitter and climb toward the light,
        feeling everything as if for the first time—

pausing stunned, stupefied with light.
    Before we, frightened by such possibilities,
        with a large wad of tissue come down on it,

and crush it until it is nothing
    but dampness and legs, an oily smear
        writing a broken Sanskrit on the paper,

a message we choose not to read
    before committing it to the water
        swirling blankly at our touch,

hoping that will take care of it,
    trying not to think of it—the dark
        from which it will rise again.

TOM SLEIGH

Shame

If only I'd known then what I was reaching for,
that my bread would haunt me
like Augustine's pears, though my theft
was nothing like Augustine's claims
that he flung his heart into the bottomless pit
because he was foul and loved his foulness;
my stealing was ordinary, unredemptive meanness,
a juvenile blindness to the cost of things
that went with my too ready, too ingratiating grin.

The refuge owner's daughter, her eyes glazed
with veiled disgust, glanced at my fingers cramped
like claws around the bread: I'd waited until everyone
had left the breakfast room, then gone basket to basket
stealing: *Why have you done this?* her eyes asked
before she turned to clear the teapots from the tables.
And what could I explain, my cheeks so swollen
with gobbled bread that I looked like one of Bosch's demons . . .

How changed I was from the day before when I'd climbed
to the refuge through slopes of boulders ground
to mica-brilliant rubble, the sun-washed meadows
incorruptibly bright, the glacier ice
above me tinged pale blue by the sky's
darker blue which seemed to pull me into it,
as if I floated in that stinging cold pure air.

The setting sun shrank back into blue-black space
shadowing ridge after ridge surging upward into peaks
that hovered one behind the other in dispersing clouds,
my eyes straining to keep it all in view—
and then across the glacier a mist unraveled like thready sleeves,
long arms lifting up and balancing in midair
ledges and crags of ice and stone . . .

But how distant that all seemed in the leaden morning light,
her eyes recoiling from my clutching hand: My breath died
inside my chest, my palms ran cold with sweat,

my shoulders hunched up around my ears: *Shame.*
I'd even felt it the night before, like a fever
coming on, when the other climbers, faces
tight with scorn for the fact that I was green, gazed
past me as I talked to them in crippled German:
They greased their boots and ordered morning thermoses
of coffee, poured Schnapps in tin cups, kept aloof
from my questions about altitude, avalanche,
crevasses . . . And then, as if my stealing
whispered that their meanness had been right,
next morning on the glacier no one spoke to me:
She must have gossiped the whole humiliating moment . . .

Her face hovered before me as I climbed,
the snowcrust's monotonous papery crunching
beneath my crampons nagging like the shame
I couldn't shake, dull
as the ache in my muscles. The summit
drifted in front of us, a fogged-in crag
high up a slope so steep that each breath came hard and ragged,
our shadows black weights dragging us back down.
I kept seeing my hand reach for the bread, the flaking
crust lightly dusted with flour, the long trestle tables
and empty benches, the teapots and coffee cups and jars of jam . . .
If only I'd known then what I was reaching for,
that her eyes would pursue me, is it almost twenty years?
The worst is knowing that I'd confirmed what they wanted
me to be—my brute confidence
that they would like me precisely, I think now,
what they couldn't tolerate: It must have rankled
to see such unconscious privilege able to buy its way
to Alpine fastnesses, though I'd labored doing shovel-work
to get there . . . no corner of the globe untouched
or wholly cordoned off . . . But could they really have lost
the war to the fathers of such sons, effeminate
in long hair? How they'd winced at the blues tune
I'd shrilled on the harmonica, thinking I'd show them
something "pure American"! In a daydream
I still have, we skirt the rim
of a crevasse, the snowcrust slides and crumbles,
our guide plunges down, down . . . the other climbers
cower while I dangle in midair, the nerve
of the rope stretching tight,
tighter as I haul him back from the abyss . . .

But of course nothing happened, the climb was sheer routine;
nothing I could do would dispel my shame rubbing
more and more raw the closer that we came to the summit . . .

The final ascent clouded to a blur of chill wind and mist. Even
the sun-flushed clouds, twisting in long chains from peak to peak,
turned leaden as they shut us in and we sank down
exhausted one by one next to the red flag snapping and shuddering.
Only for one moment did we get a view: I looked
down the slope, trying to trace
the trail I'd made, my steps receding as if flying from
her eyes that ached in my brain as bright as the sunspots
momentarily burning through the muscling clouds
and glowing on the trampled snow. The others celebrated
by drinking spiked coffee, chests swelling as they linked
arms for photographs, their voices strangely hollow
as they rehashed the climb . . .

                    At last our guide,
while disdaining to look at me, offered me
a cup of coffee (on the way back down, when we stopped
for lunch, he joked in earshot of everyone, while I fingered
my bread I was too ashamed to eat, "*Bon appetit, bon appetit!*").
Homesick among the click of camera shutters,
the tin cup burning against my mittened hands, I saw
that in his eyes I was nothing but a thief . . .
—To think *that* summed me up, my hold
on myself loosened by a stranger's
slyly scornful glance, the "I" I thought
I was mutable as mist . . . Suddenly the glacier seemed
minutely active, crisscrossed beneath the snowcrust
by a thousand cracks and fissures. Queasy before
the maze of tracks weaving down
the slope, I muttered to him thanks,
but he only turned his back, my too eager grin
freezing on my face. All around me our ice-axes
stuck blade-up in the snow, like a flock of steel birds
balanced on one leg, chill beaks dully gleaming.
—I lowered my eyes, I was seized with such shame;
and when he passed the log book, for a moment
I considered signing a false name, some anonymous John Doe
whom he could muse on later with the refuge owner's daughter,
each reminding the other, if they ever think of it at all,
The American, remember, who was the thief?

DAVE SMITH

The Egret Tree

Ghosts of our fathers flocking down at dusk,
    one by one you return and stand
  shouldering the dim western light. Limbs
      you stride, live oak chambers,
  creak with hundreds of you, white-robed
      abrupt as stars, or the flared

    windows of offices where clerks gird
for war, lawyers blue-eyed in their suits who
    peck in their own sluffed shit.
      What do our people need?
  Dusk-wind sifts the tree moss beard-gray
      in its fingers. Over the lake's

lull, past black roofs where we bend above meals,
    you descend as if elected upon this
  day, swirl to this tree, ease to a brother,
      take on your light-weight. Black
  truly comes as we visitants drawn car
      by circling car wait for a last

    bark-ragged oblivion to close upon you.
Somewhere they decide to help us, the kick stand
    of the cop's motorcycle gouges dirt,
      but we move nose to nose bent
  to know what keeps you so calm. Little
      wonder water fills with *Amens*

threading the burst last red spatter of the sun,
    then our breath stops as we wait to see
    what we never have: where you go
      fabulous as love, beauty
we must dream like this tree rooted in the mind's
      hunger, the lake's quick ooze.

Out Whistling

Driving home I see the white heron on one leg
      yards out in the lake, like a woman
sun-glazed, dreaming next to a seaside rail.
      The lifted knee, down-delicate, holds
light in my mind so I drive around the block

to find its black eye again. The little globe
      orbits with me, hidden in my car,
all of us waiting, and traffic steadily rasps
      like breath over cancered tissue.
What did you want from me? No ripple comes as

one leg replaces another, the eye satin, hard
      with moons I can't see. So much
love flashes there I remember a wind-flared
      instant, your cigarette, a street
you crossed to find me when I was out whistling.

Fieldswirl, October

Fog so thick the cows beyond the fence slide
      in and out of focus as I follow
the dogs, the morning's metastasizing ooze
      eating first light, then meat,

yet still the dragons loom through dewlens
      dropped by flying spiders, each
humped, iridescent spine spewing the steam
      nightdreams dragged to bed, stars

hurled off-orbit like a cat struck by a car. It's
      cattywampus, grandmother said, who
stood in the leafthick to thump it still, and I
      all afternoon sat boiled by sun,

sure I knew I was in hell's hold. Then I saw
      the bull pass in pines, moonlord
of life who kept the fields whole, and I slept
      distant as God from my only home,

unable to answer for the guttings, lies, slicks
      of tears crows racketed around me.
A bare world woke me. Winter, naked crabapple.
      A voice. Movement. Dawn's wiry walk.

Pulling a Pig's Tail

The feel of it was hairy and coarse
like new rope in Johnson's
hardware store but I never touched
it or any part of a pig
until that day my father took me
where the farm was, woods
a kind of green stillness, the hanging
leaves from so much rain
I guess—it felt as if I was upside
down underwater trying to swim
for my life. The farmer, Uncle Bern,
said I could have one
if I could catch it. A little one
looked easy, about my size,
wary because he must have been unsure
of many things and hungry
because the small lives always are so
I chased him until foul mud
was all over me, the big men crying.
My father said it was just
that funny like a kind of gray soul
testing to see I wanted
badly enough to catch myself, black
eyes not seeming to watch,
on the horizon sort of—the weird way
I talked to it and finally it
listened to something and I took
hold, pulled, held, grunting,
digging my sneakers into the shit. Why
wouldn't he bite me? I almost
got that thing straight but then saw
what wasn't right, the hurt.
Let go. I didn't say I was thinking
about school that was over

that summer, the teacher that yanked
my hair, who said she'd see
my life was straightened out, Lord.
I couldn't tell my father
a pig's tail burns you like all things
of beauty. I loved my school
until that wet day when it let me go.

Moles in Spring

Home from school my daughter's curled
to hide from pain, the grub
of her body knee-to-cheek enfurled

at the center of her shadowed room.
Something's scuttling in her,
little claws of hurt without home

or past or destination, that blunt
passerby she cannot welcome,
like the mole she ferried for us

bright years back, its dog-licked hide
a knot of pain, a sore
with one so comely and fair, the kind

to dazzle any wild thing with a look.
For her yellow-hair slipped
like a gown at temple, and hooked

by the flashed outflying eyes, I
myself have melted in grass
where cardinals pranced, the sly

watch they kept no barrier at all.
We played in hay, black birds
barking, and around the sun rolled

until we fell limp and listened.
Just under the edge went
the humped tunnels, dark's green

mysterious miner, the one I said
I heard, almost, and she,
clever as ever put down her head

in dirt's hold, blinked, lay open
all the looks she had, held
deep in that sweet breath and, oh,

yes, she cried, he's back for me,
who didn't die, or go away.
Undead, where is that Spring we dreamed

there'd be a harm to handle moles,
a keep-safe of all we'd sown?
Now I dream of arms. I want to kill

a beast's claws and snout and homing bone,
all stepping darkness near.
Yet how to know which is the one,

I asked the mother of my love? Oh,
cried she, just watch is all,
and listen as love does. You'll know.

Today it's spring again, the dirt is
dark, my girl folds in herself,
and over the lawn come owlish cries

from boys bumbling in dusky lights.
I wish they would go home.
I wish more the mole would gag and die.

GARY SNYDER

Night Song of the Los Angeles Basin

             Owl
       calls,
          pollen dust blows
       Swirl of light strokes writing
       knot-tying light paths,

       calligraphy of cars.

Los Angeles basin and hill slopes
Checkered with streetways. Floral loops
Of the freeway express and exchange.

       Dragons of light in the dark
       sweep going both ways
       in the night city belly.
       The passage of light end to end and rebound,
       —ride drivers all heading somewhere—
       etch in their traces to night's eye-mind

       calligraphy of cars.

Vole paths. Mouse trails worn in
On meadow grass;
Winding pocket-gopher tunnels,
Marmot lookout rocks.
Houses with green watered gardens
Slip under the ghost of the dry chaparral,

       Ghost
       shrine to the L. A. River.
       The jinja that never was there
       is there.
       Where the river debouches,
       the place of the moment
       of trembling and gathering and giving
       so that lizards clap hands there
       —only lizards

come pray, saying
"please give us health and long life."

      a hawk,
      a mouse,

Slash of calligraphy of freeways of cars.

      Into the pools of the channelized river
      the Goddess in tall rain dress
      tosses a handful of meal.

      Gold bellies roil
      mouth-bubbles, frenzy of feeding,
      the common ones, the bright-colored rare ones
      show up, they tangle and tumble,
      godlings ride by in Rolls Royce
      wide-eyed in brokers' halls
      lifted in hotels
      being presented to, platters
      of tidbit and wine,
      snatch of fame,

          churn and roil,

      meal gone   the water subsides.

      a mouse,
      a hawk,

The calligraphy of lights on the night

      freeways of Los Angeles

      will long be remembered.

      Owl
calls;
      late-rising moon.

Raven's Beak River at the End

Doab of the Tatshenshini river and the Alsek lake, a long spit of
gravel, one clear day after days on the river in the rain, the glowing
sandy slopes of Castilleia blooms & little fox tracks in the moose-print
swales,
& giant scoops of dirt took out by bears around the lupine
roots, at early light a rim of snowy mountains and the ice
fields slanting back for miles, I find my way

> To the boulders
>   on the gravel in the flowers
> At the end of the glacier
>   two ravens
> Sitting on a boulder
>   carried by the glacier
> Left on the gravel
>   resting in the flowers
> At the end of the ice age
>   show me the way
> To a place to sit
>   in a hollow on a boulder
> Looking east, looking south
>   ear in the river
> Running just behind me
>   nose in the grasses
> Vetch roots scooped out
>   by the bears in the gravels
> Looking up the ice slopes
>   ice plains, rock-fall
> Brush line, dirt sweeps
>   on the ancient river
> Blue queen floating in
>   ice lake, ice throne end of a glacier
> Looking north
>   up the dancing river
> Where it turns into a glacier
>   under stairsteps of ice falls
> Green streaks of alder
>   climb the mountain knuckles

> Interlaced with snowfields
>   foamy water falling

Salmon weaving river
  bear flower blue sky singer
As the raven leaves her boulder
  flying over flowers
Raven-sitting high spot
  ear in the river, eyes on the snowpeaks,
Nose of the morning
  raindrops in the sunshine
Skin of sunlight
  skin of chilly gravel
Mind in the mountains, mind of tumbling water,
  mind running rivers,
Mind of sifting
  flowers in the gravels
At the end of the ice age
  we are the bears, are the ravens, are the salmon
In the gravel
  at the end of an ice age

Growing on the gravels
  at the end of a glacier
Flying off alone
  flying off alone
  flying off alone

Off alone

KATHERINE SONIAT

A Last Warm Day

Shucks flit the horizon,
then turn earthward

for this late October day
where everything seems on the move—

crows circling
move their black fleet off

past the cut cornfield.
The plodding land turtle

tries for another side of it.
The other side of the road

will do just fine. Squirrels
scamper, the hesitant ones bled

into the highway by cars,
those steady weapons, so unlike

the zig-zagging pursuits
of the morning dog

who cornered the snapping turtle
on his way from ditch to pond:

big turtle caked with bullrushes,
the stench of time, his thick neck

and claws older than any
Moses in the marsh.

Even the fish are headed somewhere,
the suicidal carp at it again,

our neighbor yelling, *that fish
is jumping up and out of your pond.*

It's a strange time, this space
of ambulatory fall fever.

I focus field glasses on the hill,
spot bear cubs stumbling off

with their mother toward high country;
four wild turkeys strut

their feathered stuff while a buck
nods antlers as if in assent.

Yesterday, a fawn followed
the neighbor's boy out of the woods

to play house-pet, sleeping on the sofa,
eating packs of Lucky Strike,

the rest of the animal world intent
on dispersal. By sundown,

flies buzz on the screendoor,
crickets joining this frail abundance.

A Shared Life

The horses nuzzle,
and the bluebirds scatter from the fence post
like Sunday's children at a picnic.
But who promised all would be this idyllic
                              with the fences up
or down—the black dog shot today, bleeding
among the farmer's dead pheasants, the brown dog
uncontrollable in his pursuit of cows,
the cows bemoaning the fenced-life
the dog charges through.

Even the dozing cattle settle
under a tree-house
                              not made by children.
Platform nailed high in a field oak,
where at night deer arrive with eyes
                                        like porch lamps snapped on
                                        in the mist
as flashlight and double-barrel shotgun
                                        plug each in turn
                                        mindless
of the limits.

And there is no end to limits: no end
                      to how the guinea hens can't
                      fly high enough, to how the pheasants
                      can't run far enough, to how the black
                      dog ran straight for the pheasants
                      and now is laid out in a patch
                      of bronze feathers, while cows
                      flee the brown dog, flee
                      in four directions like the simpleminded
                      or an early fall wind, the animal warden
                      speeding across the beeline of 311 North
                      to say he don't want to cause nobody
                      no heartbreak, but those two dogs
                      broke the law; and behind him by noon,
                      comes the woman in the gray sedan,
                      taking a skiddy turn up to the dead
                      dog's porch to yell that the radio's so loud
                      it's spooking her cows. Oh, woe

unto all these dismal marriages in the fields,
woe to those with the vacant
                              or intelligent brown eyes,
to those with talons, canines or cuds.

Even on calm days, cows press their hides
to the barbed wire,
                      like noses to the window—
                      a wish, perhaps, to be one of the lost,
to be one of those with secret paths in sunlight,
hidden compasses for midnight.
A wish not to be

one of these cows who rush
each dawn ahead of this dervish of a dog,
every breath a puffed remnant

of those lost to the fog a year at a time—
our animal universe tail to mouth
tumbling into a rosy, beastly oblivion.

MARCIA SOUTHWICK

The Magic Broom

Walk out into the fields without looking behind you.
If you see an owl tearing a rabbit with its claws,
close your eyes. A woman will pluck a golden hair from her head
and throw it to the ground. It will make a twang
like the vibration of a guitar string. She's not your real mother.

Beware of snakes living in the roots of trees.
When your cap falls off and you are visible again,
snakes will surround you. Hit them with sticks.
They'll tie themselves in knots, hissing as they disappear.

You'll recognize your real mother by the black thread
in the shoe of her right foot. You'll recognize your father
by his questions: What has one eye, an overcoat of polished steel,
and a tail of thread? What has four feet and feathers,
but is not alive? What walks without feet, beckons
without hands, and moves without a body?

Don't answer. Otherwise, he'll say, "I have eyes of flame,"
and your clothes will light on fire. You'll be condemned to roll
over and over in the dust until the last spark goes out,
and that could take years. Take this scarf, unroll it,
and a river will appear between you and your father.
If he crosses, take this hairbrush, shake it, and a forest will grow.

If he follows your tracks, draw a chalk circle,
and wait for him to step inside it. Then wave this handkerchief,
and the circle will become an island in the middle of a lake.
Now you can walk home. If you want to stay fatherless, though,
carry this broom—to sweep away each footprint behind you as you go.

The Waves

The waves break against the shore with the force
of false promises. Are they giving lectures?

Will they drone on and on like they did in the old days
before our lungs took their first breath,
before our skeletons were here to start a little history?
A streak of blue cuts through my attention,
the sky reminding me that I should look outward,
not inward at my own ruins, where everything I know
is squeezed into a few crumbling walls of limestone
dissolving beneath the pressure of years.
Are the water's little nervous breakdowns a sign
that I'm falling apart? Will my self-deceptions,
half-buried in sand, be uncovered as the tide lowers,
leaving behind shells and bits of broken glass?
Why have I trusted this entourage of shadows
that follows me after each change of address?
It's as if the shadows have voted me out of office,
and I'm no longer the candidate that best represents
their vague yearnings and subtle outrage—
they'll forever remain half-formed,
colorless imitations of the things they follow,
and like the wind wringing its hands, they'll never be visible.
As I walk here, haunting the afternoon, my voice
stuck in my throat, I worry that the Gods,
performing their subtle calculations,
will cancel me out of the equations.

WILLIAM STAFFORD

Gaea

Our earth, the whole of it, is alive, they say,
like a plant or animal, each part in touch
and reaching so that the whole survives.
In such a life, in even a selfish act,
you contribute, and the world says, "Thanks, goodby."
So, often, while the barn braces itself
to hear the wind I stand quietly
all alone and read the hay.

Or, sometimes, not to know, but to spend
the time learning, I make the guitar say
a certain tone again and again
till it all adds up and becomes
what God intended from my part
of the world today. Then I pause,
and what follows that sound I make is music.

Such times, I almost know what the world
keeps telling me. It's the birds and a certain
other hum just beyond. It's the sound
the sun makes when it finds gold.
Everyone, stop whatever you're doing
and listen.

Entering a Wilderness Area

Let air discover who you are, deliver
that message for bear, for deer. Pass on
quietly, no badge needed. Pay the forest
first, then woman or man.

Below any mountain resolve your allegiances
and mention them often, like a salute no one
requires. No one need know which path
you consider but never declare.

Somewhere there's the law greater than a uniform,
not any certain color, only a code
riveted in boulders too deep
to discover. You will obey it.

No boundary can stop you.
No woman. No man.

Spirit of Place: Great Blue Heron

Out of their loneliness for each other
two reeds, or maybe two shadows, lurch
forward and become suddenly a life
lifted from dawn or the rain. It is
the wilderness come back again, a lagoon
with our city reflected in its eye.
We live by faith in such presences.

It is a test for us, that thin
but real, undulating figure that promises,
"If you keep faith I will exist
at the edge, where your vision joins
the sunlight and the rain: heads in the light,
feet that go down in the mud where the truth is."

> *(on a plaque in Portland's City Hall, for
> Portland, Oregon's, city bird)*

Kolob Canyon

The storm is coming because
    Navaho sandstone has lasted
    four hundred million years,

And because the sun throws
    powerful rays against bulwarks
    too lofty to believe.

Clouds are contending again
and shepherding snow through passes
only an angel could guard.

If you stop and face what buffets you,
a splinter of evening will penetrate
all through the life you brought here.

And the soft gray will move near,
then tower up and close in,
saving you from those giants in the sun:

To face the spirits alone,
even for an instant that stretches
out toward forever, is too much—

That is why evening steals
past the angel and surrounds you.
That is why the storm comes.

GERALD STERN

Birthday

It is that they spend so much time in the sky
that bluebirds have streaks of red across their chests;
and it is that—except for the robbing of their houses—
they came north for my birthday bringing the light
of southern Texas with them. Every year
I am able to do the mathematics
and stand like another bird—outside my door—
with one foot in and one foot out, half-looking
for the first light and whisper one phrase or other—
one or the other—and look for a streak of red
and a flash of blue. If you asked me what I lived for
I'd say it was for knowledge; I'd never say
I was waiting to see the sun come up
behind the willow; or I'd say I was living to see
the bluebirds come east again; I'd never say
I was waiting for justice, or I was waiting
for vengeance and recovery; I'd say
I was waiting to see the thumbnail moon
at five o'clock in the evening, or I was waiting
to see what shape it takes by morning or when
it becomes an acorn moon. I'd never say
the bluebird has disappeared from the east, the starling
has driven him out; I'd never turn to the starling
and the English sparrow and hate them for their stubbornness—
how could I as a Jew?—I'd never say
the pigeon is our greatest pest; how could I
who came from New York City myself? I'd say
it's too late to go to Idaho and sight
the distance to the pole; I'd say I'll never
move now to southern Arizona—I'd let
the forest come back to Pennsylvania. I am
half-English when it comes to trees; I live
for the past as much as the future—why should I lie?
I am ruined by the past. I can trace
my eyelids back to central Asia.
                              It is
when the thaw comes and the birds begin to swell

with confusion and a few wild seeds take hold
and the light explodes a little I lie down
a second time, either to feel the sun
or hear the house shake from the roar of engines
at the end of my street, the train from North Dakota
carrying sweeteners to Illinois, moving
forward a single foot, then backwards another,
one of those dreary mysteries, hours of shrieking
and banging, endless coupling, the perfect noise
to go with my birthday, grief and grinding enough,
wisdom enough, some lily or other growing
on the right of way, some brakeman still wearing a suit
from Oshkosh, he and I singing a union song
from 1920, some dead oppossum singing
something about a paw-paw tree, his hands
over his eyes, some bluebird greased with corn oil
and dreaming of New York State singing songs
about the ruins or about the exile, notes
from southern Texas, notes from eastern Poland,
drifting into the roundhouse, Lamentations
of 1992, a soft slurring
on her part, a tender rasping on mine,
though both of us loving the smell of mud, I think,
and both of us willing to snap some twigs, although
for different reasons I think, and both of us loving
light above all else, almost a craving
that occupied our minds in late February
and made us forget the darkness and the wobbling
between two worlds that overwhelmed us only
a month or two before. It has to be
the oldest craving of all, the first mercy.

Ducks Are for Our Happiness

Ben Franklin again, down by the esplanade
watching the green ducks flapping, eating a bagel
from Bruegger's, sipping his coffee, eating his heart
out again, remembering spring after spring—or was
it love after love. He feels like a fool, in spite of
his letters. He likes the face of the mallard, he finds it
sweet, and quizzical. He loves when the sun shines

directly on the neck; he loves how the mallard
cleans itself; he tries to bend his neck
and rub his beak on the feathers. He is angry
because of his loneliness; he likes the head
going back and forth; he likes the speed. It is
the warmest day yet. If he could sit here an hour
he would be happy. "Ducks are for our happiness,"
he says in a letter to Fresno. "They resolve
our fear of separation." I am reminded
constantly of Sappho, how the heart
in her ribs shook with misery, how her tongue
was broken and her eyes were dead to the light.
"But he is determined," he says to Fresno, "to put
sorrow on the other burner." He is
disgusted with lovers' moping—at his age—
restless thoughts—and slouching—"he who started
with a bun," he says to Fresno, "ends up with a package
of day-old bagels." He tosses a piece of poppyseed
to one thin duck whose head goes back and forth
as if it were on a spring. He spreads cinnamon
among the sleepers. He curses what has happened
to Jewish bread, but then he settles in
to watch the ducks until it gets cold. His river
is narrow now, it once was huge, he barely
could see across—it seemed to rise in the middle—
and when the thaw came there were sometimes trees,
and deer, and sofas, floating by; this river
is more like a small canal, even the bridges
are small here, but he likes how it turns on itself
as if it still were looking for its outlet,
and that's something. He finishes his letter
and brushes the crumbs off. One green duck pursues
him, it is his own voice shrieking; it stands
its ground—like a dog—it is the way that grief
stands its ground; fear and sadness combine
to make him like that. He rubs his own neck raw—
for this is *his* weakness—and dips his bill in water
to try to get his strength back. Franklin, dear Fresno,
tries to pet the duck and ends up running
down the esplanade in reckless pursuit
of his own voice, of a brawling duck
angry beyond belief, moving sideways
into the bushes, sliding into the river

to get away, carrying the anger with him,
cries of irksomeness, agitations, dark
nights of the soul; arranging the transfer to him
of another's unhappiness, the water of misery
he swims in; as Franklin arranges the Ethics and studies
the slats on his bench. The ducks would die for him,
if they had to, they are magic. Is it the oil?
Is it the feathers? And how do they know his oddities?
He walks between two bridges talking French
to his youngest sweetheart, he has written her letters
in two languages, she read to him at night
and fixed his pillows. She, of all his loves,
he longs for most; he wants to watch her again
bend her head to the ground as she brushes her hair,
he wants to bring her chocolate, he hates loneliness
and he hates anger disguised as pity. "He could
write about it," he tells the ducks, "dejected
facial expressions, vain imaginations,
even whimpering." The ducks only sing.
My God, that is their singing. "Think of that,"
he tells no-one, "think of the ducks singing;
my God, their warbling, their near notes and their far notes;
their low-pitched chucks; their musical trills, their whistles,"
he says to the river. "My God, their happiness, Fresno!"

Bitter Thoughts

I didn't listen to one stone this year
or one drop of water. I climbed my arborvita
and held on for dear life. My foot was always
too big and here I was in my sixties freeing
one leg again. It was always that. One bush
was reddish brown. I loved the color but hated
the stiffness. One house was blowing such dirty steam
I thought it was my childhood again. The stone

was blue at the base, half from the river, half
from the slate inside. It faced the island. Moss
of some kind grew on top. If it were a mountain
there would be wind, there would be a branch. What was it
that made me moan like that, that made me touch

the vein above my left ear and reduce
the pain through thinking, through *thoughts* to be exact,
bitter thoughts. I was on a train

to be exact, I was going back to New York
from Philadelphia—I was reading Horace;
a fire had started somewhere in the cable
or in the rubber underneath. There was
a little smoke already. We were hurried
forward; the train was rushing through New Jersey
and rocking from the speed. The light was sputtering
and I was reading and rubbing the vein above

my left ear. The pain was leaving. I could feel
it leave. That was yesterday, the end
of January, 1991; today
the sun is out. The train got to New York
and I was in my apartment in twenty minutes,
not one minute more. I sat in my coat
looking out the window, I couldn't see
details, but I only wanted the shape

and nothing more—maybe a little sky
between the top of my window and the roofline.
I notice today, sitting in my bathrobe,
how large the trees are—I had to look through the branches
to see the sky, but I don't remember; one fence,
of all the fences, is made of wood and there is
ivy growing over it, there are flagstones
behind one building and there is a charcoal burner

with last year's charcoal still intact behind
another. Not one goat. I was never
a tree-climber, though more from fear of heights
than from the size of my foot but I was up high enough
to see the river and see the lapping without
hearing it. The island was out of sight
from where I stood—I could have hung from the limb
and seen the tip of it, if I could climb

out of my heavy shoes, if I wasn't frozen
with fear. The stone was one of those stones for thinking.

It had a seat. The hand went up to the chin
naturally. It was surrounded with sand
and there was a stick to help you, some dry twig
lighter than air, something so soft it broke
as soon as you pressed it a little. It was the fire
though that set me thinking, and it was Horace

that set me drifting. There is a poem he wrote
about a trip to Brindisium. I read it
once or twice a month to get the secret.
I worry that I have *created* him, that he is
not that modern, but every time I read it,
although I know it now by heart and *say* it
rather than read it, I want to be sitting there
drinking new red wine with the Roman poets

and turning some skinny thrushes over the fire
rather than sitting by a window alone
in New York City, counting branches. His day,
or so he said, always ended by eating
a little cereal and going to sleep; it was
a good meal for a poet. My day ended,
at least today—yesterday—by racing
into the station at top speed, bypassing

Newark, as I remember. I was standing
between the cars, the plates were turning, we were
hanging on—and coughing—there was something
exhilarating in it; maybe New York
was being delivered; maybe disease was withdrawing
and no-one will die untimely, maybe pain
and hatred will be unknown, maybe mosquitoes
will leave their holes and minister to children.

My driver was Haitian; he believed felicity
will cover the earth. He only charged me four dollars
so I had something left for breakfast. The bird-bath
I loved the most and the rows of chimneys second,
though nothing could beat the dead leaves on the trees
or the canvas chairs. I could find the stone,
if I had to, and the tree. The island is drowned
in garbage now; the river is ruined. I put

one orange on a dish, that is a sign; I turn
the lock two times. Just going down into the street
I am revived—I am sweetened. The foreign
and bitter are here. I love them always; but I have to
be alone upstairs. There is a bookcase
lying on the sidewalk; I'll come back
in an hour to pick it up. I know the wood
is almost split; words have ravaged it. Who
could have thrown it out? Next year, next January,

maybe I'll find a harp, or the end of a lute
with a wire attached, maybe the wind will sing
for me—there on a granite curb—and maybe
knowledge will come and I will understand it
once and for all, the light that first existed, the
struggle between imperishables, what I thought of
for most of a life, near a water-stained lampshade
that saved the world and an overcoat that renewed it.

ANNE STEVENSON

Salter's Gate

For Peter

There, in that lost
    corner of the ordnance survey.
Drive through the vanity—
    two pubs and a garage—of Satley,
then right, cross the A68
    past down-at-heels farms and a quarry,

you can't miss it, a T instead of a +
    where the road meets a wall.
If it's a usual day
    there'll be freezing wind, and you'll
stumble climbing over the stile
    (a ladder, really) as you pull

your hat down and zip up your jacket.
    Out on the moor,
thin air may be strong enough to
    knock you over,
but if you head into it
    downhill, you can shelter

in the wide, cindery trench of an old
    leadmine-to-Consett railway.
You may have to share it
    with a crowd of dirty
supercilious-looking ewes, who will baaa
    and jerkily run away

after posting you a mad stare
    from their boxy pupils.
One winter we came across five
    black, icicle-crowned cows.
But in summer, when the heather's full of nests,
    you'll hear curlews

following you, haunting your memory, maybe,
        with their eerie cries;
or, right under your nose,
        a grouse will whirr up surprised,
like a poet startled by a good line
        when it comes to her sideways.

There are no—well, very few—trees.
        Hawthorn the English call May,
a few struggling birches.
        But of wagtails and yellowhammers, plenty,
and peewits who never say *peewit*,
        more a minor, *go'way, go'way*.

Lots of clouds, soot-purple like the sheep,
        though sometimes fleecy enough,
Blake's lambs grazing
        light blue fields in his Jerusalem?
Not at Salter's Gate.
        They raise animals to eat in England's Durham.

Salter. Who was he? Why was this his gate?
        Maybe the base root's *saltus*,
Latin for leap. The place has a feeling of
        survival, its unstoppable view,
a reservoir, ruins of the lead mines, new
        forestry pushing from the right, the curlew.

Cold

> There is something very serious and
> fundamental about cold.   —Philip Larkin

Snow. No roofs this morning, alps, ominous message
        for the jackdaws prospecting maps of melt.
Something precipitates an avalanche;

a tablecloth slips off noisily
        pouring heavy laundry into detergent,
a basin of virgin textiles, pocked distinctively

with ice crystals. Your shovel violates this *blanchissage*
    with useful bustle, urgency pretends;
but it's helpless as the swallowed road on which

the air lets fall again a lacier
    organza snow-veil. Winter bridal
the muffled dog fouls briefly. *Don't the cedars*

look beautiful, bent under clouds of fall?
    And it's true, time has no pull
on us; we set it aside for another

"very serious and fundamental" briefing:
    chaffinches at the birdfeed, a sentinel
jackdaw on exposed slates, the worried men

tiptoeing their accelerators, deepening
    very carefully each other's ruts.
As if—for how long?—matter had beaten them

and the cold were bowing them backward to—
    or forward to—a steadier state. Ice
sets in and verifies the snow.

Imagine a hidden rule, escaped from words,
    stealing the emergency away from us,
starving the animals eventually; first, the birds.

Level Cambridgeshire

its islands of England
apportioned by drain
and motorway,

dolls-house villages
that have lost their childhood,
roses called "peace"

and "blessing" exclusive to
frilly white cottages and
pie-crust thatch,

with rustic muscular black
beams so charmingly
depended on,

spiked like St. Sebastian
with a heritage
of nails . . .

Can you hear it?
The wind
or traffic. The low-hummed

roar of the hundred-ton
saurian lorries and a
soughing avenue of

18th century limes sound
the same.
In another film

the heroine escapes with
the hero into rural
Cambridgeshire

circa 1509. A field of
barley, feathered; a fen full
of sky-blue

butterfly flax with
undulations like
the ocean's

rolling right up to the
cameraman's pollen-dusted
loafers.

And when Anthea sets up
her easel to catch
a picturesque

angle of the almshouses in
watercolour, she
scrupulously omits

electrical wiring and
TV paraphernalia that,
in strange time,

connect her to
"the brutish, uncivilized tempers"
of these parts,

the cottagers' corpses
stinking and unburied
by the furrows,

Christ's men in retreat
at the Fever House
at Malton,

there "to tarry in time of
contagious sickness at
Cambridge

and exercise their learning
and studies" until
such time as

God pleased to make
the city safe again for commerce
and superior minds.

Painting It In

(Remembering Lesley Parry)

Wake up at six o'clock. We're out to sea.
Nothing beyond that fence and slatted gate
but a grey wave and plume-like shapes that could be
flaws in the canvas or unmixed pigment in paint.

Quotations from Camden's *Britannia*, Gibson's edition; see G. M. Trevelyan, *English Social History*, 1948, 3rd edition, p. 148; and from *An Inventory of Historical Monuments in the County of Cambridge, West Cambridgeshire*, Vol. 1. (Royal Commission on Historical Monuments, England, 1968).

Stones, blurred poppies, a wheelbarrow full of grass
affirm a foreground. The world must exist out there.
People must be getting up and getting washed,
putting the kettle on, picking up a newspaper.

Somewhere it must matter terribly not to be late,
not to miss the limousine to the airport,
not to be missed when the finance committee votes;
when the training course commences, not be left out.

But somewhere is hard to believe when it's not invented,
when the world blindly refuses to admit detail.
All that's required is pastoral: sheep among stunted
rowans; for background, eroded 'Moelfre' or 'bald hill.'

The thing's been done so many times. Imagine
brushing the lichen's pearly quartz over the rocks,
now the shocking pink foxgloves, painting them in,
old fashioned *belles de joie*, drunk on their stalks.

What if today decides never to take off its veil,
never to palliate art with a grand show
of perspectives up the valley? More likely all we'll
get is light's first lesson, an application of gesso,

a whiteout of air—sweet, soft, indestructible,
the cloud of unknowing reluctant to create the known.
Hills, stones, sheep, trees are, as yet, impossible.
And when things are unmade, being also feels less alone.

MARK STRAND

Here

The sun that silvers all the buildings here
Has slid behind a cloud, and left the once bright air
Something less than blue. Yet everything is clear.
Across the road, some dead plants dangle down from rooms
Unoccupied for months, two empty streets converge
On a central square, and on a nearby hill some tombs,
Half buried in a drift of wild grass, appear to merge
With the houses at the edge of town. A breeze
Stirs up some dust, turns up a page or two, then dies.
All the boulevards are lined with leafless trees.
There are no dogs nosing around, no birds, no buzzing flies.
Dust gathers everywhere—on stools and bottles in the bars,
On shelves and racks of clothing in department stores,
On the blistered dashboards of abandoned cars.
Within the church, whose massive, rotting doors
Stay open, it is cool, so if a visitor should wander in
He could easily relax, kneel and pray,
Or watch the dirty light pour through the baldachin,
Or think about the heat outside that does not go away,
Which might be why there are no people there—who knows—
Or about the dragon that he saw when he arrived,
Curled up before its cave in saurian repose,
And about how good it is to be survived.

DABNEY STUART

Desolation

At the top of the dune
the wind blew with such force
he could not turn into it.
Sand filed the sides
of his windbreaker hood,
making a little tunnel downwind
of his head he looked into.
He was all
but lifted up.
Had he turned and not been
blinded he would have seen
a row of jars in the sand,
each holding a translucent
foetus, the lustrous dark
eyes calling
his unborn names.

Palm Reader

The end of my life
hops into my hand
like a grasshopper in a dry field.
If I were going to fish with it
I would close my hand
over it and place it in a jar
with some dry grass in the bottom
and air holes punched through the lid.
At dusk I would thread my hook
through its collar just behind
its curved black eye, or run the hook
up through its throat and out its mouth,
carrying a brown bubble on the tip.
Cast into the placid, twilit pool
it would twitch on the surface
as if it belonged there and could drift

until it reached the bank
and leapt back into the field
and into my hand again.
If I were simply curious
or gone into another phase where fishing
was a boyhood silhouette and my wrist
didn't remember the rod tip's
delicate motion, I would watch it
interrupt the lines in my palm:
vaguely reptilian with its yellow-
brown armor plating, the upper leg
chevronned, the lower with its rows
of fine barbs, thin as a needle.
It could be taken for a calm,
meditative vestige of another time,
or simply an insect terrified to poise
by this alien surface it's lighted on.
I could say it looks back at me.
If I could see with its eyes
I would become a mosaic of light
and shadow, colored in some way
complementing the background I seem
to emerge from, or blend with.
I would be as still and complex
as it is, and it would live in my hand.

Figure on the Edge

Gillespie Beach, NZ: The Tasman Sea

He looks as if he's a silhouette
cut from one medium and glued on
another, a slim print
of someone's artistic finger, a sharp
nonce. The expanse
of numberless stones composing
the beach—the sea's shambles, geologic
toejam—makes
a wide strip at the bottom.
He walks on it.
The sea and the sky are close enough
to what one usually expects

in photographs, or at the shore,
to be taken for what they look like:
curled surf, the clouds dazed in light.
There are two places to go, then,
either toward the implacable line called
horizon, which no one reaches, or
into the other depth, the flat dark
that becomes the man walking
on the flat dark of the beach,
feet and stones lost in it,
the outline of his body forming
the only space he could fall into.

Rumination

The cowbell sounds
in the redolent field,
its dinted clack cupped
by the 5 AM fog
rising, hung
laundry in the rifted air.
The blunt clapper
in its pocked copper
well carols
the morning, rings
clean in its campanile,
sounds to who knows
what creature dreaming
in the mistlifted woods
or holding a match
toward the edge of
an old map, tinder
for a new lost life, sounds
who knows
what creature
                    in whose flutter
of being
a membrane begins to hum,
catching,
            letting
its unlikely music flare
into the open.

ERIC TRETHEWEY

Florilegium

Nodes of light on the table,
they glowed for almost a week,
daisies and asters and whatnot,
sensing in the air around them
noise of an alien tongue,
though living still in the language
of where they came from.

We gathered them one by one
by the side of the road,
up in rockhill pastures,
or down along the creek.
And we brought them here
to brighten habitation
with news of a fresher world.

Today they are stooping stems,
faces folding in on themselves.
Like the eye of day closing
at dusk, or the stars put out
by clouds, by heavy weather,
they are nothing to us now
but drying husks, their names.

Resurrection at West Lake

Ringed by dark palisades
of spruce and this cold, black
bowl of water, I understand again
about words, how folded wings

can open, lift into flight:
love, when it batters us,
or *death*, when we sense its swoop,
a wendigo stirring in shadows.

This one-crow sky leans on my bowels.
My eyes are admonished
by witch fingers of naked poplars
forming their mute adjurations.

And social voices fall silent too:
crows, chickadees, whiskeyjacks
contain their clatter; squirrels
grow mute as pinecones.

Up on the ridge behind me
thin, bone-white remnants
of the deepest snowdrifts glow,
skeletal under the hackmatacks.

Out of these enigmatic evergreens,
around imponderable granite mounds,
beneath one flapping black rag
of crow, spring's surge begins again.

Reading the Signs

Intent upon meaning, we mean
in time, as lovers do, to forge
our final sense of things.

But today we tramp along the creek
in search of local epiphanies
instead—moments so full of themselves
(green aureoles around their leaves)
no instant is left over for outcomes.

Though *now* always turns
into *then*: we know we'll arrive
at trees gaunt with November,
moments when nothing stalks up
to the edge of things,
each object abandoned to itself,
remote in hard-edged clarity.

This has a cold glory all its own,
though it doesn't last either,

complications unavoidably on the way—
such as what is offered down the road
in the glances strangers exchange
along busy streets,
the civil passage of untidy news.

Life speaks to us—all these little
things we are never done with.

Near Dawn

Tugged out of bed by a dream,
he enters the world, confronts
cats stalking the hallway,
aghast at this early walker.
The moon, almost full, glows
on the crust of old snow.

Back in the bedroom, his wife
dreams in a world that is his
to return to. Perhaps.
But for now he's here
by the window, moonlight
glazing the earth.

He is watching five foxes
drift through the yard, gather
for a moment by the pear tree,
sniffing the air, inquisitors
out in the cold. They turn to what
beckons higher up on the ridge.

Ghost Birches

The road crew worked all afternoon
cutting the dead birches.
Run-off from the road salt killed them,
trapped as they were on the narrow strip
left between the asphalt and the lake,
and rain-weakened. The acid
starts the yellow inflammation early,
the leaves in June already
arthritic in the cells.
We used to call them snow ghosts:
one white hidden in another.
Now they're stacked in six foot sections,
their branches trimmed away,
and in the lake
the new emptiness heals over.
Then comes the plow of winter
straight down the valley,
pushing its wedge-shaped shadow.
All the lesser shadows move aside
as if still talking to one another,
flexible in wind, accessing their losses,
the future already upon them,
its sky-blue speckled crystals burning
down through the packed snow into the earth.
Maybe a man on the crew
with a truck of his own
will come on Saturday
to haul the white logs away, cut and split
and stack them, and he'll find them
crumbled to embers in his stove
when he comes home late and cold
from plowing after a heavy snow,
their shadows having already slipped
up the chimney to join all the other
shades of the world, the young ones
gone back to lie beside their stumps,
the old ones free to travel anywhere.

Dirt

I was standing in the frozen garden
spreading wood ashes, wondering
about the space in which music plays,
how it also gets recorded,
and the dirt in a record's grooves,
the scratchy, friendly, pre-tech sound of it,
like waves almost, a frictional circular
crosscurrent, a counterpoint.
I had been reading my will,
writing my whims in the margins
in pencil, just fooling around with ideas
about the dispersal of my property,
part of which I was standing on.
Who would most love to put down
one of my books and come outside
to stand here on the frost-crusted soil,
the mountains already casting
their blue winter shapes
down into the valley?
If age is a measure
of the world's weight in us,
I'll someday fill to overflowing,
a little flood of dust,
and will then lie intimate with dirt,
or be blown in the form of ash
into the cells of the blossoming woods.
There I was,
looking down at the remnant stalks,
collapsed tomato skins,
horse manure still in its rounded
tea-colored briquets, like petrified grass,
a sort of vegetable fossil.
I don't want to die, but all knowledge
leads to the one conclusion, after all.
Suddenly the will with its silly ribbons
and wax seal seemed nothing but
an inventory of delusions,
instructions to my survivors
for the time when I'll become
the soil riding in the black grooves,
the compost layered with leaf-ghosts,
a crumb of what I was when I was alive.

The Immortal Pilots

The noise throws down
twin shadows, hunting shadows
on a black joy ride.
They roar up the silver
vein of the river
and out over the Adirondack Range,
which has been shrunken
to a luminous green
musculature on their screens.
Who are the pilots,
too high to see
the splayed hearts of deer tracks
under the apple trees, or smell
the cider in the fallen fruit?
Who are the vandals that ransack
the wilderness of clouds?
Below them, a thin froth of waterfall
spills from a rock face.
They see its sudden wreckage,
its yielding gouts,
and the wind tear into the papery
leaves of the poplars,
roughing them up
so the undersides show—
a glimpse of paleness
like a glimpse of underwear.
The pilots are young men,
and still immortal.
Already in the cold
quadrants of their hearts
they imagine the whole world
flowering beneath them.
It feels like love,
like being with a woman
who flowers beneath them,
so that they wonder
how it would feel to go on
riding the young green world that way,
to a climax of spectral light.

Snow in Condoland

I enter the orchard at nightfall
when it's hard to tell
the clots of late spring snow
from the apple blossoms,
the dead from the living,
though the mind has no trouble
with snow as a flower,
snow as a corsage
it can press inside its heavy book.
I could go on turning the pages
forever, so vivid
are the images there,
so perfectly preserved.
Their forms grow vaguer in the yards
as the slow light falls on swingsets,
paved cul-de-sacs, mailboxes,
doghouses, acres of cold cars,
the whole stilled ocean of roofs.
The orchard has been gone
for a decade, and still the sentences
push through the laden branches,
into each frozen complex
of white on white.
It's fascinating, isn't it?
The way language smudges and erases
and redraws what it wants for itself?
Even now the apples
are ripening somewhere,
inside the cold petals maybe,
in the dark, still infant part,
where a faint pink fever
was once supressed.

MONA VAN DUYN

Poets in Late Winter

for Joe Summers and Albert Lebowitz,
Birdwatchers

I.

The poets of Missouri stare at astonishing winter.
On the windshields of their disabled cars they can see
rain, snow, hail, sleet, fog
all at once. Only the river still runs with pity.
The white sandwich they live on is snow between slabs of ice.
For three weeks no one can walk. Perhaps
sold-out salt will float in, they can sit beside
their stricken friend, iced in without guides or maps;
throw enough friction under their skidding souls
to pick up the news thrown on their own front yard
(One man who fell and lay helpless outside his door
clutched his paper and bellowed to wake his lifeguard,
who hunted the house up and down for her husband's voice);
can carry hot food to the trembling next-door widow
(self-immured for ten days from the poisonous glass)
without a steel-point stave to poke down to snow
while wearing golf shoes to crack-step across the lawn;
can send a serious verse to the humorist
who smashed her thirty-year-old hip. For three days
no mailman comes. Never was mail more missed.
Books and small screen pall, poems that hail
into the cold mind coldly rattle like ping-pong.
In St. Louis seventy mailmen are hurt in falls
the day they try again. It goes on too long.

After two weeks the poets of Missouri hear
that their wintering-over birds are going to die.
For too long the inches of ice on top of snow
on top of ice have kept them from seeds, though they fly,
searching everywhere, through the freezing storms.
Each dried-berry-hung bush is iced off from a bill.
There is no water, each pond and stream stays solid.

Such innocent song to suffer the earth's ill-will!
In city, village, farm, frantic, the poets
set out to save the lovely reds and blues
of cardinal and jay, the cocky mocker,
junco, chickadee, waxwing . . . pulling their golf shoes
on and off all day, they balance warm water
again and again, fill feeders, their mittens smeared
with peanut butter, fat, raisins, breadcrumbs.
From wind and sorrow their face-scarves and eyes are teared.
And the little ones come from the woods, at least some, bedraggled,
too starved and thirsty to scare when food is thrown,
sparrows and starlings too, crows, pigeons, everybody.
Old bird books wake and call out birds unknown.
In his bright beret even the huge red-bellied
woodpecker hunches down to the holes of the feeders.
"If we stick together," he says to the poets of Missouri,
"The earth will re-print for its most devoted readers."

        II.

The poets of Missouri, in color, are dreaming
a T.V. drama that troubles their sleep:
when they sailed to these shores of being and seeming
they were met by a giant in exquisite motley
who became their faithful servant. Whatever
they asked he brought or did, though he
was mute except for a high little hum
(as he went about his magical work)
which they took to be happiness. Bang of drum
and now he appears, arms at his side,
dressed like a robot in Reynolds Wrap.
He is looking at them. Used to the big wide
billboards of human grief and desire,
they're unable to understand such a look.
Next a zoom to his heart. If he should aspire
to a heart, they supposed it crisp, firm, green
like a Granny apple. But what runny chaos
is this that erupts all over the screen?
Whatever it was is now worn, rancid,
its form weakened by lack of care,
lack of gratitude, praise. Amid
its weary, mushy straining to live
are runnels of need and pain. Their paper

feelings crumple as they cry, "Forgive . . ."
How *could* they have guessed that the generous monster
loved them? The camera shifts and he turns
transparent. Heart fills his throat like fur.
"Our word, our world," they cry, "we've been wrong!"
He tries to hum again, but chokes up
and ends that tiny, unearthly song.

MARILYN NELSON WANIEK

Abba Jacob and St. Francis

Abba Jacob with his invention—
a flashlight lantern on a cord around his neck—
balances tiptoe on an upended barrel.
There's one,
he mutters, and reaches.
The damned creatures
are making lace
of my arbor.
He holds the beetle for a moment,
then breaks it and tosses it aside.
The seculars watching,
laughing, tease him:
So much for St. Francis.

Abba Jacob says:
Well, at least I don't call them
brother
and *then* kill them.

But I do
ask God's pardon.

Dusting

Thank you for these tiny
particles of ocean salt,
pearl-necklace viruses,
winged protozoans:
for the infinite,
intricate shapes
of sub-microscopic
living things.

For algae spores
and fungus spores,

bonded by vital
mutual genetic cooperation,
spreading their
inseparable lives
from Equator to pole.

My hand, my arm,
make wide sweeping circles.
Dust climbs the ladder of light.
For this infernal, endless chore,
for these eternal seeds of rain:
Thank you. For dust.

ROSANNA WARREN

The Cormorant

for Eunice

Up through the buttercup meadow the children lead
their father. Behind them, gloom
of spruce and fir, thicket through which they pried
into the golden ruckus of the field, toward home:

this rented house where I wait for their return
and believe the scene eternal. They have been out
studying the economy of the sea. They trudged to earn
sand-dollars, crab claws, whelk shells, the huge debt

repaid in smithereens along the shore:
ocean, old blowhard, wheezing in the give
and take, gulls grieving the shattered store.
It is your death I can't believe,

last night, inland, away from us, beyond
these drawling compensations of the moon.
If there's an exchange for you, some kind of bond,
it's past negotiation. You died alone.

Across my desk wash memories of ways
I've tried to hold you: that poem of years ago
starring you in your *mater dolorosa* phase;
or my Sunday picnic sketch in which the show

is stolen by your poised, patrician foot
above whose nakedness the party floats.
No one can hold you now. The point is moot.
I see you standing, marshalling your boats

of gravy, chutney, cranberry, at your vast
harboring Thanksgiving table, fork held aloft
while you survey the victualling of your coast.
We children surged around you, and you laughed.

Downstairs, the screen door slams, and slams me back
into the present, which you do not share.
Our children tumble in, they shake the pack
of sea-treasures out on table, floor, and chair.

But now we tune our clamor to your quiet.
The deacon spruces keep the darkest note
though hawkweed tease us with its saffron riot.
There are some wrecks from which no loose planks float,

nothing the sea gives back. I walked alone
on the beach this morning, watching a cormorant
skid, thudding, into water. It dove down
into that shuddering darkness where we can't

breathe. Impossibly long. Nothing to see.
Nothing but troughs and swells
over and over hollowing out the sea.
And, beyond the cove, the channel bells.

Man, That Is Born of Woman

It is in slow choking
that leaves flare.
And that single spider strand
flung between shrubs
catches nothing
but sun splinters.
Each leaf an hour:
look, look, the hours
shudder against the regulation blue.
Warm palm on granite:
it's only my own
pulse cantering
as it did against your
cold and stiffening hand.
All around me, life
grips: the oak-leaf stem
holds hard the throttling twig,
lichen and moss seize
the Precambrian ledge, wild

grapevine strangles
the beech: my
hand, gripping
this granite glacial
shelf, could clench as surely
an altocirrus wisp,
as freely
let it go.

Song

        A yellow coverlet
        in the greenwood:
spread the corners wide to the dim, stoop-shouldered pines.
        Let blank sky
        be your canopy.
Fringe the bedspread with the wall of lapsing stones.
        Here faith has cut
        in upright granite
"Meet me in Heaven" at the grave of each child
        lost the same year,
        three, buried here
a century ago. Roots and mosses hold
        in the same bed
        mother, daughter, dead
together, in one day. "Lord, remember the poor"
        their crumbling letters pray.
        I turn away.
I shall meet you nowhere, in no transfigured hour.
        On soft, matted soil
        blueberry bushes crawl,
each separate berry a small, hot globe of tinctured sun.
        Crushed on the tongue
        it releases a pang
of flesh. Tender flesh, slipped from its skin,
        preserves its blue heat
        down my throat.

RICHARD WILBUR

A Wall in the Woods: Cummington

1.

What is it for, now that dividing neither
Farm from farm nor field from field, it runs
Through deep impartial woods, and is transgressed
By boughs of pine or beech from either side?
Under that woven tester, buried here
Or there in laurel-patch or shrouding vine,
It is for grief at what has come to nothing,
What even in this hush is scarcely heard—
Whipcrack, the ox's lunge, the stoneboat's grating,
Work-shouts of young men stooped before their time
Who in their stubborn heads foresaw forever
The rose of apples and the blue of rye.
It is for pride, as well, in pride that built
With levers, tackle, and abraded hands
What two whole centuries have not brought down.
Look how with shims they made the stones weigh inward,
Binding the water-rounded with the flat;
How to a small ravine they somehow lugged
A long, smooth girder of a rock, on which
To launch their wall in air, and overpass
The narrow stream that still slips under it.
Rosettes of lichen decorate their toils,
Who labored here like Pharaoh's Israelites;
Whose grandsons left for Canaans in the west.
Except to prompt a fit of elegy
It is for us no more, or if it is,
It is a sort of music for the eye,
A rugged ground-bass like the bagpipe's drone
On which the leaf-light like a chanter plays.

2.

He will hear no guff
About Jamshyd's court, this small,
Striped, duff-colored resident
On top of the wall,

Who, having given
An apotropaic shriek
Echoed by crows in heaven,
Is off like a streak.

There is no tracing
The leaps and scurries with which
He braids his long castle, ra-
Cing, by gap, ledge, niche

And Cyclopean
Passages, to reappear
Sentry-like on a rampart
Thirty feet from here.

What is he saying
Now, in a steady chipping
Succinctly plucked and cadenced
As water dripping?

It is not drum-taps
For a lost race of giants,
But perhaps says something, here
In Mr Bryant's

Homiletic woods,
Of the brave art of forage
And the good of a few nuts
In burrow-storage;

Of agility
That is not sorrow's captive,
Lost as it is in being
Briskly adaptive;

Of the plenum, charged
With one life through all changes,
And of how we are enlarged
By what estranges.

The Self-Defense of Peaches

The new peach trees are bandaged
like the legs of stallions.

You can read the bark
over the tape's white lip

where its russet braille
is peeling. The peaches hang

in their green cupolas,
cheeks stained with twilight,

the wind stenciled on velvet
livery. What a traffic

of coaches without wheels,
of bells without tongues!

Far off the barn doors
open, close,

open, close.
An argument,

both sides swinging.
The blue tractor zippers the field

and disappears behind slatted boxes
like weathered shingles, stained

with peach-juice.
I stood under peaches

clumped close as barnacles,
loyal as bees,

and picked one
from the only life it knew

and the whole tribe rolled
over me.

A Little Blessing

After an hour's climb, I am no closer
to Peter Wing's house. I don't doubt
(scuffing my way along the vineyard path),
that somebody is keeping me in sight.

The pond and vineyards don't belong to him
but to the wealthy man who owns the valley.
The one-strand fence that lassos Peter's field
keeps milkweed and a knock-kneed pony in

and keeps me out. Why do I balk at lines
like latitudes, defenseless against loss?
Between the shorn vines, a milkweed bows
under the blue machinery of heaven.

Below the Catskills stenciled on blue air
darkness is washed and shaken out to dry,
Vines drape their ponderous swags across the hill
and creatures hoofed and horned, bristled or bare,

lie down and thank the great eye of the night
and Peter Wing for keeping us in sight.

In Praise of the Puffball

The puffball appears on the hill
like the brain of an angel,
full of itself yet modest,
where it sprang like a pearl
from the dark fingers of space
and the ring where light years ago

it clustered unnoticed,
a gleam in the brim of Saturn,

a moon as homely as soap,
scrubbed by solar winds
and the long shadows of stars
and the smoke of dead cities
and the muscles of the tide
and the whorled oil of our thumbs,
and the earth, pleased to make room
for this pale guest, darkening.

The Wisdom of the Geese

The geese are displeased.
They want to invent the snow.

Each has swallowed
a whole pitcher of light.

Stuffed with brightness,
they can hardly move.

As they waddle through tall grass
they drop feathers, quaint clues,

like the arch humor of ferns.
Something wakes the pond, wrinkling it.

It's bad luck to look back.
They step off into dark water.

CHARLES WRIGHT

Reading Lao Tzu Again in the New Year

Snub end of a dismal year,
                                    deep in the dwarf orchard,
The sky with its undercoat of blackwash and point stars,
I stand in the dark and answer to
My life, this shirt I want to take off,
                                    which is on fire . . .

Old year, new year, old song, new song,
                                    nothing will change hands
Each time we change heart, each time
Like a hard cloud that has drifted all day through the sky
Toward the night's shrugged shoulder
                                    with its epaulet of stars.

————

Prosodies rise and fall.
                        Structures rise in the mind and fall.
Failure reseeds the old ground.
Does the grass, with its inches in two worlds, love the dirt?
Does the snowflake the raindrop?

I've heard that those who know will never tell us,
                                    and heard
That those who tell us will never know.
Words are wrong.
Structures are wrong.
                        Even the questions are compromise.

Desire discriminates and language discriminates:
They form no part of the essence of all things:
                                    each word
Is a failure, each object
We name and place
                        leads us another step away from the light.

Loss is its own gain.
                        Its secret is emptiness.
Our images lie in the flat pools of their dark selves

Like bodies of water the tide moves.
They move as the tide moves.
                              Its secret is emptiness.
                              ———

Four days into January,
                    the grass grows tiny, tiny
Under the peach trees.
Wind from the Blue Ridge tumbles the hat
Of daylight farther and farther
                              into the eastern counties.

Sunlight spray on the ash limbs.
                              Two birds
Whistle at something unseen, one black note and one interval.
We're placed between now and not-now,
                              held by affection,
Large rock balanced upon a small rock.

Looking outside the Cabin Window, I Remember a Line by Li Po

The river winds through the wilderness,
Li Po said
            of another place and another time.
It does so here as well, sliding its cargo of dragon scales
To gutter under the snuff
                        of marsh willow and tamarack.

Mid-morning, Montana high country,
Jack snipe poised on the scarred fence post,
Pond water stilled and smoothed out,
Swallows dog-fighting under the fast-moving storm clouds.

Expectantly empty, green as a pocket, the meadow waits
For the wind to rise and fill it,
                              first with a dark hand
Then with the rain's loose silver
A second time and a third
                        as the day doles out its hours.

Sunlight reloads and ricochets off the window glass.
Behind the cloud scuts,
                              inside the blue aorta of the sky,
The River of Heaven flows
With its barge of stars,
                    waiting for darkness and a place to shine.

We who would see beyond seeing
                    see only language, that burning field.

Winter-Worship

Mother of Darkness, Our Lady,
Suffer our supplications,
                         our hurts come unto you.
Hear us from absence your dwelling place,
Whose ear we plead for.
                    End us our outstay.

Where darkness is light, what can the dark be,
                              whose eye is single,
Whose body is filled with splendor
In winter,
               inside the snowflake, inside the crystal of ice
Hung like Jerusalem from the tree.

January, rain-wind and sleet-wind,
Snow pimpled and pock-marked,
                         half slush-hearted, half brocade,
Under your noon-dimmed day watch,
Whose alcove we harbor in,
                    whose waters are beaded and cold.

A journey's a fragment of Hell,
                         one inch or a thousand miles.
Darken our disbelief, dog our steps.
Inset our eyesight,
Radiance, loom and sting,
                    whose ashes rise from the flames.

Mondo Henbane

The journey ends between the black spiders and the white spiders,
As Blake reminds us.
                For now,
However, pain is the one thing that fails to actualize
Where the green-backed tree swallows dip
                         and the wood ducks glide

Over the lodgepole's soft slash.
Little islands of lime-green pine scum
Float on the pot-pond water.
                    Load-heavy bumblebees
Lower themselves to the sun-swollen lupine and paintbrush throats.

In the front yard, a half-mile away,
                    one robin stretches his neck out,
Head cocked to the ground,
Hearing the worm's hum or the worm's heart.
Or hearing the spiders fly,
               on their fiery tracks, through the smoke-choked sky.

GARY YOUNG

Four Poems

I

I don't know where the owls go when they leave this place, or if they never leave, but simply leave off calling sometimes in their hollow voices. But tonight they are here: one in a redwood beyond the creek, one high in the fir tree above the house. Rappelled through their voices, those three long vowels the darkness speaks in, I forget my own worthlessness which has troubled and chastened me all day.

2

Our son was born under a full moon. That night I walked through the orchard, and the orchard was changed as I was. There were blossoms on the fruit trees, more white blossoms on the dogwood, and the tiny clenched fists of bracken shimmered silver. My shadow fell beside the shadow of the trees like a luster on the grass, and wherever I looked there was light.

3

Where deer tracks enter the stream, the water's erased them. Bay leaves and oak leaves drift along. It's autumn, and everything seems to be falling away. Even that old bitterness has left me. The crayfish have lost their shells. They walk backward through the shallows, their new skin so vulnerable, translucent, and blue.

4

I watched a snake crawl onto the lily pads that cover the pond. A fish settled against the leaf, just beneath him. All that afternoon, they never closed their eyes. They barely moved. I still may lose my disaffections and impatience with the world. I may rest.

PAUL ZIMMER

Another Place

You come to a place in winter woods
That seems remembered, a foundation full
Of rusty tools, door knobs, dog bones,
Peach stones, scissors, where hard winds
Blew for years through blackened timbers.
Small wings of frost still strive on weeds,
But so many things are missing now,
Pervasive regret has assumed the place.
You feel fine snow flitter down
And settle into the ancient residue,
Gathering in cockle burrs, ear holes,
Joints of aspen, sockets of your eyes.
Slowly it begins to change you into
Something better than yourself.

Crazy with Love

Crazy with love, the birds fold
Over each other and tie knots
Right in the middle of roads.
They sit around in greenery
Ogling and pecking each other,
Sweet talking stridently,
Their titillation makes blossoms
In trees sprinkle and sing.

How can you keep good sense
With all this loop and flash,
Ponder serious career moves
Or forward knowledge in
Some weighty manner with
This feather-brained high jinx
Swirling around your head?

It's enough to make you flap
Your sore, grinding arms
And blare like a ga-ga crow,
Crazy enough with love to
Start some board-legged dance
And twirl until you tear a muscle.

for Julian and Sylvia Wolff

What I Know about Owls

They can break the night like glass.
They can hear a tick turn over in
The fur of a mouse thirty acres away.
Their eyes contain a tincture of magic
So potent they see cells dividing in
The hearts of their terrified victims.
You cannot hear their dismaying who,
You cannot speak their awesome name
Without ice clattering in your arteries.

But in daytime owls rest in blindness,
Their liquids no longer boiling.
There is a legend that if you are
Careful and foolishly ambitious,
You can gently stroke for luck and life
The delicate feathers on their foreheads,
Risking always that later on some
Quiet night when you least expect it,
The owl remembering your transgression,
Will slice into your lamplight like a razor,
Bring you down splayed from your easy chair,
Your ribcage pierced, organs raked
From their nests, and your head slowly
Rolling down its bloody pipe into
The fierce acids of its stomach.

The Brain of the Spider

For a moment concentrate on a spider's brain,
The various colored segments of its matter:
Crimson for power, blue for balance,
Green for judgment, yellow for cunning.
Think how it inspires the shape of dew,
How it squares frost and causes
The silver sweep of its filaments to
Stroke your face in woods and streets.
Regard the air it fixes between strands,
Its careful allowances for time and space.
Then consider what is most complex:
The unnerving grayness of its patience,
White speed of its sudden charges,
The raven segment it maintains for death.

ROBERT PACK

Afterword: Taking Dominion
over the Wilderness

The origin of humankind's ambivalence toward nature can be located metaphorically in the Book of Genesis. The language that describes the six days of divine creation is filled with wonder and awe, and God's assertion of the goodness of His creation anticipates what will follow from God's creation of creatures capable of praise and celebration. In the first account of God's creation of human beings, both male and female are created in God's image, unlike the second account, in which Eve is created from Adam's rib. The initial account is followed by God's first commandment, "Be fruitful and multiply," but this imperative is succeeded by a second one—"subdue [the earth], and have dominion over the fish of the sea, and over the fowl of the air, and over every living thing that moveth upon the earth"—which will prove to be antithetical to the first.

The second commandment, to subdue and take dominion, is a projection of the human wish to possess and master and, beyond a certain limit—a limit our species confronts today—is not in harmony with the spirit of celebration and appreciation. Adam's taking dominion over nature will be followed, after the Fall, by Adam's taking dominion over Eve, and that will be followed by Cain's taking dominion over Abel by murdering him. This split in human desire between seeking to give praise and seeking to take dominion, accelerating vastly in the age of industrialization and technology, has led to the current ecological crisis.

The morality inherent in the commandment to be fruitful and to multiply, which concurs with the innate evolutionary imperative to promote survival and has served that purpose well, has, nevertheless, brought about a paradoxical fate. We have reached the point at which to succeed is to fail, for if we continue to multiply as a species at the current staggering rate, as we are programmed to do by our genes and our biblical morality, we will defile our space and exhaust our resources in a short time. This rampant increase in population, leading inevitably to widespread famine, is likely to prove irreversible. Our only hope is to reinvent ourselves in light of a new psychology, which understands that a fruitful world is not one in which the multiplication of one species, our own, causes the annihilation of other species. What this prognostication means, then, is that we must devise a new morality of restraint, a curtailment of the wish encoded in our genes to replicate themselves— a morality not of domination but of sharing, not of acquisition but of aesthetic appreciation, not of species' self-idolatry but of reverence for a world of diverse forms of life. A renewed sense of beauty will have to replace the longing for power as the heart of human motivation. Such a morality is fundamentally the opposite of what we have taken to be our species' biblical and genetic injunction to procreate. It is the purpose of this essay to consider our predicament today, largely through the eyes of poetic metaphors, in its evolutionary context.

The immemorial idea of the vastness and inexhaustibility of nature needs to be replaced with the idea of the finiteness and vulnerability of nature, for the commandment to subdue nature never assumed that nature could indeed be subdued and replaced by human creation and human culture on this delicate planet. If nature's evolutionary plenitude is superseded by human creation, then there will be nothing outside ourselves worthy of reverence and awe. Taking dominion over nature, finally, means that we will have nothing left but our species-centered self-idolatry to be inspired by and to worship. The ultimate irony of our assuming the role of "God" is that it already appears that we may replace ourselves with our own superintelligent machines. Perhaps that is a consummation devoutly to be wished, for surely it would be folly to assume that evolution stops with us. Even if we assume that the desire to preserve human nature reveals the nostalgia of human beings for their own kind, this allegiance represents our deepest feelings about what is valuable and thus gives meaning to our lives. When the primary models for beauty and creativeness no longer are grounded in nature, we will already have evolved into another kind of species. Though we can predict and imagine where new technologies might take us, we have not begun to conceive the new values that would replace the sense of beauty and the capacity for empathy.

In appreciating nature, in giving thanks in the spirit of awe for its incredible beauty, its diversity, its evolutionary history, however, we need to beware of sentimentality and thus to keep in mind nature's cruelty and indifference. To the extent that taking dominion over nature has meant that wilderness has been tamed and cultivated into orchards, farms, and gardens, where fruitfulness continues to be honored, then subduing natural forces still can be seen as a good. But the full appreciation of the images of the farm and the garden depend on the awareness that we have made something from materials that have preceded us, whose divine or evolutionary creation are wondrously beyond us and on whose substance we necessarily depend.

The awareness of the need for balance between the wildness of untamed nature and the human cultivation of nature is exemplified for the modern American imagination in the writing of Henry Thoreau, who, though arguing in his influential essay "Walking" for the essential human need for wilderness, "The most alive is the wildest," also acknowledges the need for human cultivation: "I would not have every man nor every part of a man cultivated, any more than I would have every acre of earth cultivated: part will be tillage, but the greater part will be meadow and forest." Thoreau at Walden Pond maintained a connection with town and with society, since he well understood that the mind, too, requires cultivation. Roderick Nash, in his comprehensive *Wilderness and the American Mind*, summarizes that for Thoreau "wildness and refinement were not fatal extremes but equally beneficent influences Americans would do well to blend." Such blending, however, never envisaged the fundamental diminishment of nature's power over humankind; it never foresaw a landscape dominated by metal, glass, and concrete; it never foresaw the pollution of rivers and the sea; it never foresaw the sky besmirched with smog and ripped by a cancer-inducing hole in the ozone. Not only is physical health associated with the need for natural wilderness, however; so too is the human spirit refreshed by this sense of otherness, this plenitude, this power beyond human contrivance: "Give me the ocean, the desert, or the wilderness!" cried Thoreau.

II

When the Lord answered Job out of the whirlwind, He presented Himself in the language of inscrutable and infinite power: "Where wast thou when I laid the foundations of the earth?" The unmistakable implication of that question is that nature is too vast to be subdued. Although this view of the Lord of nature is both humbling and frightening to Job—since divine creation and destruction are inextricably bound—the poem's implicit optimism is that despite the failure of human longing to find meaning and justice in the design in physical reality, nature nevertheless is of infinite beauty and value. Job's mortality and smallness in relation to a universe indifferent to his personal anguish takes on meaning because Job sees himself as part of an unfathomable design, and therein lies Job's affirmation of his creaturehood, his resignation to his role in nature—which has dominion over him.

Job's wish never to have lived—"Let the day perish wherein I was born"—is a perverse version of the desire to be immortal, the wish not to be bound by the basic law of nature that nothing survives, that all matter, organic or inorganic, undergoes change. The rejection of that hopeless wish to achieve godhead, which results in Job's acceptance of his own mortality, is synonymous with Job's affirmation of nature's having dominion over him. In this sense, Job, as Adam's inheritor, has reconciled himself to Adam's and Eve's punishment for desiring forbidden knowledge and power, to extend the wish to take dominion over nature to dominion over life itself. Adam and Eve were banished from the garden, the emblem of natural bounty, because their wish for immortality was antithetical to natural limits. The Lord sends them into exile, both physical and psychological, when He casts Adam out "lest he put forth his hand, and take also of the tree of life, and eat, and live forever," for Adam's bloated desire to seize dominion has proved fatal. Job's reconciliation, his acceptance of human limits, becomes a model for us to emulate as our numbers, like a spreading cancer, continue to abuse the exhausted earth that has mothered us, now that we have reached the critical limit that the earth can sustain, a limit that we could not believe existed.

Just as nature in the Book of Job is represented by God's voice in the whirlwind, His extended descriptions of the weather—"Who cuts a path for the thunderstorm / and carves a road for the rain— / to water the desolate wasteland, / the land where no man lives; / to make the wilderness blossom / and cover the desert with grass"—and His detailed portrayal of the animals He has created—"Do you deck the ostrich with wings, / with elegant plumes and feathers? / She lays her eggs in the dirt / and lets them hatch on the ground"—so too the power of nature in Homer's *Odyssey* is represented by the sea, particularly the storms at sea, which will destroy all of Odysseus's fellow sailors. Odysseus is introduced to the reader as a man who has "weathered many bitter nights and days / in his deep heart at sea," a man singled out for enmity by the sea god Poseidon:

> Yet all the gods had pitied Lord Odysseus,
> all but Poseidon, raging cold and rough
> against the brave king until he came ashore
> at last on his own land.

The angry forces of nature are not the only cause of Odysseus's prolonged suffering and the destruction of his men; rather, as Homer makes clear, it is the men's "own recklessness destroyed them all— / children and fools, they killed and feasted on / the cattle of Lord Helios, the Sun." Their disregard for nature, their violation of nature's sanctity, finally brings about their ruin. Much later (Book 12), after Odysseus's men have committed the crime of killing the Sun god's "peaceful kine," Lord Helios asks Zeus for retribution, threatening to withdraw his nurturing light from the living world and "go down forever / to light the dead men in the underworld." Zeus placates Helios and, like Poseidon, turns against Odysseus's men:

> Peace, Helios: shine on among the gods,
> shine over mortals in the fields of grain.
> Let me throw down one white-hot bolt, and make
> splinters of their ship in the winedark sea.

Thus, Zeus's will is enacted, and Homer, in a fatalistic tone, concludes: "No more seafaring / homeward for these, no sweet day of return; / the god had turned his face from them."

In opposition to the imagery of nature as flux, to nature as a destructive and adversary force, Homer counterpoises the enduring power of art and the symbol of solidity and longevity, the marriage bed, which Odysseus had carved out of the trunk of an olive tree. The carved marriage bed, an emblem of Odysseus's finally taking dominion over his own instinct for wandering, is the culmination of the numerous instances in which art is extolled by Homer. For example, when the minstrel at the palace of Alkinoos (Book 8) sings the story of the fall of Troy, the usually poised and canny Odysseus is so moved that he "let the bright molten tears run down his cheeks, / weeping the way a wife mourns for her lord / on the lost field where he has gone down fighting." Although Alkinoos empathizes with Odysseus's emotion, he says:

> Tell me why you should grieve so terribly
> over the Argives and the fall of Troy.
> That was all gods' work, weaving ruin there
> so it should make a song for men to come.

This extreme claim that life and suffering should become subject material for song and story asserts that the flux and brevity of nature can be redeemed through the power of memory as preserved through art. So too, when Odysseus in revenge is massacring the suitors (Book 22) and is about to slaughter them, the court minstrel, Phemios, thinks first to protect his precious harp:

> . . . But first to save
> his murmuring instrument he laid it down
> carefully between the winebowl and the chair,
> then he betook himself to Lord Odysseus,

clung hard to his knees, and said: "Mercy,
mercy on a suppliant, Odysseus!
My gift is song for men and for the gods undying."

Odysseus, in effect accepting Alkinoos's claim, spares Phemios for the sake of his art.

The order of art may be seen as antithetical to the destructiveness of nature, yet the source of art is to be found in nature itself, as the primary emblem of order-bestowing art, Odysseus's bed, makes manifest. Thus, nature is seen as providing the substance for art out of its own (mothering = *mater*) material. Odysseus's description of the bed confirms his identity, and through Odysseus's meticulous and loving description, Penelope knows for certain that Odysseus has returned to her:

There is our pact and pledge, our secret sign,
built into that bed—my handiwork
and no one else's! An old trunk of olive
grew like a pillar on the building plot,
and I laid out our bedroom round that tree,
lined up stone walls, built walls and roof,
gave it a doorway and smooth-fitting doors.
Then I lopped off the silvery leaves and branches,
hewed and shaped that stump from the roots up
into a bedpost, drilled it, let it serve
as model for the rest. I planned them all,
inlaid them all with silver, gold and ivory,
and stretched a bed between—a pliant web
of oxhide thongs dyed crimson. There's our sign!

The transformed trunk of the olive tree, made of what endures in nature, becomes the sign of marriage, the art of human constancy, and this constancy in love is the closest Odysseus or any man can come to achieving immortality.

But it is not Odysseus's fate to die at home in the bed of his own design; it is his destiny to return to the sea, to the nature against which he had pitted himself. When Odysseus had descended to the underworld (Book 11) to receive a prophecy from Tiresias, he was told what trials and sorrows awaited him if Helios's kine were violated, and he was instructed to make a sacrifice to Lord Poseidon. He was assured then that although he would die at sea, nevertheless, it would be a peaceful death; this "seaborne death" symbolizes Odysseus's final acceptance of nature as a force to which human control and human art must give way:

. . . Then a seaborne death
soft as this hand of mist will come upon you
when you are wearied out with rich old age,
your country folk in blessed peace around you.
And all this shall be just as I foretell.

And so, in acceptance of nature and the death that nature exacts, Odysseus, like Job, will die a peaceful death, honored and reconciled to the fate that he shares with all other natural creatures.

III

Perhaps the most comprehensive work of the human imagination in depicting the rival claims of responding to nature's power and beauty in the spirit of dread and awe, on the one hand, and the power of taking dominion, of human cultivation and control, on the other, is Shakespeare's late play, *The Tempest*, which Leo Marx, in *The Machine in the Garden*, claims "may be read as a prologue to American literature." The storm in *The Tempest*, like the sea in Homer's *Odyssey* or the whirlwind in the Book of Job, is an agent of both destruction and renewal, and Prospero's power for goodness derives precisely from his ability to simulate a storm and thus to take dominion over it. Miranda, at the beginning of the play, does not understand Prospero's uses of nature. In saying, "Had I been any god of power, I would / Have sunk the sea within the earth," she reveals her wish to eliminate the destructive element, which nature can transform only by employing its own power.

To comprehend Shakespeare's balanced attitude toward nature in this play, we must consider, in addition to the imagery of the storm, the relationship between Ariel and Caliban, both inhabitants of the island before Prospero. Both can be seen as symbolizing the primal forces in human as well as external nature, but it should be noted that Caliban's witchlike mother, Sycorax, when pregnant with Caliban, was banished from "Argier" (Algiers) and deposited on the island by sailors. Unlike Ariel, Sycorax is not original to the island, and Shakespeare's implication may well be that natural beauty and creativity are forces older than greed and murderousness. At the turning point of the play in act 5, Prospero chooses to forgive his treacherous brother, Antonio, rather than indulge himself in the dark pleasure of revenge; he does this, however, at the hint and gentle prodding of Ariel:

ARIEL: . . . your charm so strongly works them,
                 That if you now beheld them, your affections
                 Would become tender.
PROSPERO: Dost thou think so, spirit?
ARIEL: Mine would, sir, were I human.
PROSPERO: And mine shall.
                 Hast thou, which art but air, a touch, a feeling
                 Of their afflictions, and shall not myself,
                 One of their kind, that relish all as sharply,
                 Passion as they, be kindlier mov'd than thou art?
                 Though with their high wrongs I am struck to the quick,
                 Yet with my nobler reason 'gainst my fury

> Do I take part: the rarer action is
> In virtue than in vengeance.

Although Ariel can be thought of as a projection of Prospero's conscience, or superego, in contrast to Caliban, who represents murderous and sexually rapacious instinct, or id, Shakespeare's metaphorical structure, I believe, presents both Caliban and Ariel as aspects of primal human nature. Their main linkage is to be found in the single virtue that Caliban possesses, which he comes by not through reason (since he considers language to be a curse) but instinctually: his appreciation of the island's natural beauty and music:

> CALIBAN: The isle is full of noises,
> Sounds and sweet airs, that give delight, and hurt not.
> Sometimes a thousand twangling instruments
> Will hum about my ears; and sometime voices,
> That, if I then had wak'd after long sleep,
> Will make me sleep again: and then, in dreaming,
> The clouds methought would open and show riches
> Ready to drop upon me; that, when I wak'd,
> I cried to dream again.

Caliban is not capable of moral understanding or empathy; for him Miranda—even though he can appreciate her beauty—is merely a vehicle for multiplying, for populating the island with more Calibans. Still, Caliban does have an innate capacity for delighting in the sensuous beauty of the island. The music that moves him so deeply, of course, is Ariel's music, which Prospero, in freeing Ariel, has put to his own moral, as well as aesthetic, uses. Ariel thus represents a beauty and harmony inherent in nature, even more fundamental than Caliban's lust and hostility. The power of art, as Shakespeare represents it in *The Tempest* through Prospero's book and Ariel's music, is not merely the human imposition of order upon chaotic force, but the human ability (as if by magic) to exploit and redirect a natural force for human purposes. Shakespeare's central paradox is that human beings cannot transcend nature without the aid of nature, whereby what may begin as a curse, nature's violence, ends as a blessing, nature's transfiguration of itself through human art. Despite Prospero's power over the elements and his own psychological nature, as represented by both Caliban and Ariel, Prospero's ultimate and consummating magic, which he achieves only through an extreme effort of will, lies in his ability to forgive his treasonous brother. Forgiveness, as in many of Shakespeare's plays, is represented as the transforming power of moral magic. The full realization of this paradox can be seen in Ferdinand's response to Ariel/Prospero's music:

> FERDINAND: Where should this music be? i' th' air, or th' earth?
> It sounds no more;—and sure, it waits upon

> Some gods o' th' island. Sitting on a bank,
> Weeping again the king my father's wrack,
> This music crept by me upon the waters,
> Allaying both their fury, and my passion,
> With its sweet air.

Just as Ferdinand is able to recognize the redemptive power of the music, so too, at the play's end, he can express wonder at the identical potentiality of stormy nature itself: "Though the seas threaten, they are merciful: / I have cursed them [as Miranda had earlier] without cause." To which the kindly Gonzalo replies, "Now all the blessings / Of a glad father compass thee about!"

Shakespeare's play explores the different meanings of servitude and freedom in bodily, psychological, and political terms, and he makes precise distinctions to show when servitude and when freedom are the appropriate conditions for particular characters. For example, Ariel, the spirit of nature and, as I have argued, of creative human instinct, was imprisoned, before the action of the play begins, by Sycorax, Caliban's witch mother. Sycorax is not a native of the island but a cast-off from human civilization; thus, she represents the destructiveness of the fallen world, of nature corrupted, of social and political evil. In freeing Ariel at the end of the play, Prospero, in effect, is removing a curse on nature itself.

Shakespeare makes it perfectly clear that Caliban's good qualities, such as his ability to perform useful work like carrying logs, will be released only when he is under the control of a proper master. Otherwise, Caliban (as we can readily see in the plot with Stephano and Trinculo) will give in to his penchant for destructive wildness, which in human beings takes the form of rape and murder. So too is servitude in the name of love a good thing, and Ferdinand accepts such servitude willingly in behalf of Miranda in obeying Prospero's order to carry logs. Ferdinand must, in a sense, pass through a Caliban-like stage, after which he will be able to recognize the paradox of freedom in accepted servitude:

> Might I but through my prison once a day
> Behold this maid: all corners else o' th' earth
> Let liberty make use of; space enough
> Have I in such a prison.

The play ends with both Ariel and Prospero, each according to the needs of his own nature, being set free. Prospero, having taught Caliban language, is now responsible for him. He fully accepts this when he says, "This thing of darkness / I acknowledge mine," and so Prospero will have to take Caliban back to Milan with him, where he can be controlled like the other rebellious and primally murderous forces, the enmity of brother against brother. In taking Caliban with him, Prospero will be leaving the island in its natural state, as it was before the interventions of Sycorax or of Prospero himself, to Ariel alone. Inviting the audience to identify with him, Prospero asks for the intervention of prayer and empathetic forgiveness when he says in conclusion: "As you from crimes would pardon'd be, / Let your indulgence set me free." In acknowledging Caliban as his own, Prospero, in effect, confesses that all the crimes committed or intended during the play are to be found in potential form within himself. Such self-knowledge is the basis of Prospero's empathy, and it explains, as well, his capacity for forgiveness. The crimes for which Prospero needs the audience's "indulgence" are those that he himself might have committed.

Prospero seeks not only moral peace at the play's end but also aesthetic peace, the rest that follows creation. The model for such needed rest is to be found in the Bible, as suggested by Ariel when he responds to Prospero's question, "How's the day?" with the cryptic remark: "On the sixth hour; at which time, my lord, / You said our work should cease." The analogy here is to God's resting after six days of creation, nature having been completed. When Prospero decides it is time to abjure his "rough magic," which he describes as "heavenly music," he withdraws his controlling hand and returns nature to itself, to its original condition of wilderness.

> . . . I'll break my staff,
> Bury it certain fathoms in the earth,
> And, deeper than did ever plummet sound,
> I'll drown my book.

While Prospero's magic prevailed, no one in the play drowns, but now that he must "drown" his book, a storm, once again, will be a storm; nature will be both beautiful and cruelly indifferent.

Ariel's freedom is closely related to Prospero's acceptance of the fact that nature both precedes and follows human art. Prospero's final words to Ariel, "then to the elements / Be free, and fare thou well!" indicate that Ariel, as elemental nature, must, in some sense, remain free of human imposition. It is right for Prospero to control Caliban, but it is not right for Prospero to exercise unlimited control over Ariel. If Ariel, like Caliban, represents not only some aspect of original nature but also some aspect of Prospero's nature, of human nature, then Ariel's freedom must mean some final liberation of human beings from consciousness, from moral thought itself, back into matter, back into the cosmic materials out of which human life emerged. Language in this play is seen both as a curse and as a blessing, but like Prospero's visionary pageant, his story and his art, words must "dissolve" back into nature, Ariel's element, out of which they came, "into air, into thin air."

The quintessential argument for the human need for wilderness may be seen as expressed in Shakespeare's dramatic vision of our little lives being "rounded with a sleep." One can make sense of human life and human values only when one perceives them as vanishing, a temporary effulgence of nature. Thus, it is nature, outlasting us, outlasting our dreams, to which we must give our deepest allegiance, not what we, in our passing, make of nature through human contrivance and human art. Without wilderness, our humanity is diminished because we fail to perceive the beauty inherent in our ephemerality; we fail to acknowledge ourselves as creatures among other creatures, among other evolving and vanishing forms.

IV

The great rebellious reader of the Book of Job, William Blake, who claimed that "where man is not, nature is barren," sought to give equal status to human creation, the power of the human imagination, to take dominion, so that God's "fearful symmetry" in creating a tiger, for example, could be balanced by Blake's creation of a tiger in which he imposes the symmetry of his own poem (the first stanza returns almost exactly as the last) on nature itself. Although the balance of power has shifted somewhat from the Book of Job, nature, in Blake, has not yet been degraded or subdued, though it surely has met both an admiring and a potent adversary. Blake identifies the human imagination and artistic creativity not with nature but with God when, for example, he claims that "all deities reside in the human breast"; yet Blake is equally aware that the imposition of human organizations, such as religion or social custom, on nature (including human instinct) can destroy the very nature that it has power to tend.

In his poem "The Garden," Blake envisions the destruction of fruitful nature, symbolized by the garden, as the result of the moralizing priests who have lost the sense of natural beauty and thus turned the garden into a cemetery "filled with graves, / And tombstones where flowers should be." And in "The Human Abstract," Blake attempts to disassociate the image of the tree as a symbol of guilt, which corrupts the mind, from the innocent tree as it exists simply in nature: "The Gods of the earth and sea, / Sought thro' Nature to find this Tree / But their search was all in vain: / There grows one in the Human Brain." In other words, the perversion of the human desire to appropriate nature, made manifest in the mind as guilt, leads to deceit and hostility, exacerbating the split in human beings between their sense of themselves as creatures of nature and their wish to take dominion over nature. Thus, Blake, though champion of the human artistic imagination, maintains original awe in the face of nature's plenitude.

Original awe in response to the inexhaustible vastness of nature pervades Wordsworth's poetry even though he has begun to worry about the encroachment of the city—"greetings where no kindness is"—on human psychology. In Wordsworth, the fear that subduing and taking dominion over nature, symbolized by the city as the exemplary human structure, becomes a central theme and a deep source of anxiety and possible despair. In the climactic scene in "The Prelude" (Book VI, lines 617–40) in which Wordsworth crosses the Alps, he has a vision of nature's infinite and eternal capacity both to create and to destroy: "The immeasurable height / Of woods decaying, never to be decayed." This vision is sublime because it is frightening and consoling at the same time: frightening in that it places all creation, including human life, under the sway of change and thus makes everything temporal and finite; consoling because it implies that the source of endless change leads continuously into further creation and new life. Ultimately, then, nature is seen as the capacity for multiplying without limit, and this consoling belief enables Wordsworth to affirm the personal limit of his own mortality. Although humankind is mutable and mortal, nature's mutability represents the divine power of its inexhaustibility from which humanity derives a sense of meaning and purpose. Beauty, for Wordsworth, is the experience of nature that enables us to find ecstatic happiness even in the awareness of our own extinction, precisely because we can connect mortality, personal limitation, with a force of continuity and innovation even beyond death.

Blake and Wordsworth, like Job, contemplated destruction, and they found ways to make peace with both the indifference and transience of nature, but they did not have to face the destruction of nature through human domination. Although poetry for them is the proper vehicle for lamentation for personal sorrow or human cruelty, the burden was not given to them, as it is to us today, to consider the replacement of natural power by human power as the primary determinant of evolutionary change, both biological and social. Blake and Wordsworth are fully aware of how deeply destructive human behavior can be in their analyses, for example, of city life, but neither of these visionaries can foresee that nature itself can be destroyed and superseded. Their faith is securely based on the assumption of humankind's limited power: we are safe precisely because we cannot take dominion over nature.

As one of Wordsworth's great inheritors, Gerard Manley Hopkins, says in "God's Grandeur," a poem about the besmirching of nature through industrialization, that "all is seared with trade; bleared, smeared with toil." Human desecration, however, has only minimal power compared to nature's power of renewal, for "nature is never spent; / There lives the dearest freshness deep down things." Yet Hopkins does provide us with the glimmering of a nightmare vision of what the world would be if nature were to be subdued, if human domination became a final reality:

> What would the world be, once bereft
> Of wet and wildness? Let them be left,
>   O let them be left, wildness and wet;
> Long live the weeds and the wilderness yet.

Hopkins's cry for the preservation of nature is raised to a high pitch of urgency, one that even Wordsworth's most passionate successors have difficulty in sustaining. Even modern war, as we see in Dylan Thomas's "Ceremony after a Fire Raid," cannot prevent nature from continuing in its process of renewal. Although a bombing raid on London causes Thomas to envision "beginning crumbled back to darkness / Bare as the nurseries / Of the garden of wilderness," Thomas's faith—the stubborn and traditional faith in an indomitable nature—leads him to proclaim nature's triumphant power of revival and renewal:

> The masses of the infant-bearing sea
> Erupt, fountain, and enter to utter for ever
> Glory glory glory
> The sundering ultimate kingdom of genesis' thunder.

For Thomas, nature never loses the power of domination in its own kingdom; it can forever re-create itself, over and over again.

V

The fundamental optimism, though deeply tinged with prophetic anxiety, of the English Romantics' and post-Romantics' attitudes toward their belief in the sovereign power of nature is carried over into the American wilderness movement and into the substantial body of nature writing in American poetry. Two central concepts that mark this transition are the idea of "correspondences," the links between nature and the human spirit, and the idea that nature is the means by which human beings maintain their connections with their origins. At the beginning of "The Prelude," for example, Wordsworth declares that "while the sweet breath of heaven / Was blowing on my body, [I] felt within / A correspondent breeze." Here, the influence of God's creative force is experienced in nature as a breeze, as if the gentle wind were the same breath that God originally breathed into Adam to give him life; this breath of nature, then, becomes the source of human inspiration.

So too does Emerson, in his essay "Nature," argue that "every natural fact is a symbol of some spiritual fact. Every appearance in nature corresponds to some state of the mind." Emerson repeats and develops this idea—"this radical correspondence between visible things and human thoughts"—culminating in his assertion that "the whole of nature is a metaphor of the human mind." The unmistakable implication of such reasoning is that the body of nature and the human body are indivisible;

any violation of nature is equally a violation of the human mind, the human spirit.

In Wordsworth, Emerson's most influential predecessor, the quest for self-identity and self-knowledge necessarily involve the search for human origins. "How shall I seek the origin?" Wordsworth asks, and, typical of the way he seeks to answer his own question is his representation of moments of looking and listening, attending to the world of natural images: "and I would stand, / If the night blackened with a coming storm, / Beneath some rock, listening to the notes that are / The ghostly language of the ancient earth, / Or make their dim abode in distant winds." Again, in listening to the winds, now in their less gentle and grimmer aspect, Wordsworth senses a connection between mere physical sounds—perceived, however, as "notes"—and human language, which has emerged from matter itself. To understand our humanity we must, according to Wordsworth, understand the medium of nature out of which language, our distinguishing human characteristic, has been born.

The worshipful language of John Muir constantly reminds us of the need to understand the mystery of human identity as growing out of, and being dependent upon, what is beyond us and what has preceded us in evolutionary time. When describing the High Sierras, Muir says: "In so wild and so beautiful a region, every sight and sound [was] inspiring, leading one far out of himself, yet feeding a building up of his individuality." So too is humankind's deepest spiritual resource, the sense of beauty, dependent upon physical imagery: "We felt our faith in Nature's beauty strengthened, and saw more clearly that beauty is universal and immortal, above, beneath, on land and sea, mountain and plain, in heat and cold, light and darkness." And Roderick Nash, reflecting on the tradition of American nature writing, considering how it has led to the "new ecology-oriented environmentalism," emphasizes the human need for connection with both the planet's and our human evolutionary past when he speaks of our need to remember "man's biological origins, his kinship with all life, and his continued membership in and dependence on the biotic community."

In American poetry also, we see the attempt to give nature its due, to respect its beauty and its power, even as we make claims for the legitimacy of culture and the goodness of giving some human order to the wilderness, since this wilderness corresponds to an animating energy inherent in human instinct. In Emily Dickinson's poem, for example, "I started Early—Took my Dog," a young woman, the poem's speaker, takes a walk with her dog to visit the sea; in her fantasizinig mind, the sea becomes her first lover and seduces her:

> But no Man moved Me—till the Tide
> Went past my simple Shoe—

> And past my Apron—and my Belt
> And past my Bodice—too—

Although the youthful speaker of the poem experiences an infantile fear of sexual violation when she says of the Tide, "He would eat me up," the language of the poem is remarkably delicate, so the speaker's anxiety is minimized, through an aestheticizing analogy, in comparing the masculine Tide to "a Dew / Upon a Dandelion's Sleeve."

The speaker turns from the sea to return home, but the Tide pursues her:

> And He—He followed—close behind—
> I felt His Silver Heel
> Upon my Ankle—Then my Shoes
> Would overflow with Pearl—

This fantasy of impregnation by nature, as personified by the Tide, comes to an abrupt conclusion in the last stanza with the confrontation of two forces (both depicted as male) of nature, embodied as the Tide, and civilization, embodied in the "Solid Town":

> Until We met the Solid Town—
> No One He seemed to know—
> And bowing—with a mighty look—
> At me—The Sea withdrew—

The opposition between nature and civilization, between lover/Sea and father/Town (as Dickinson said of her father: "his heart was pure and terrible"), appears to pit each against the other as irreconcilable adversaries. The father/Town's failure even to recognize the lover/Sea suggests the immense repression of nature as an aspect of the self that comes as the result of the attempt to dominate nature. Dickinson's poem ends with a tactically deferential gesture: nature withdraws. The poem's concluding inference is that the Sea, according to the rhythm of the Tide, will return, and so too will the sexual urges that have been awakened in the mind of the initiated speaker.

In the poetry of Robert Frost too, nature is seen both as seducing and as threatening. In Frost's poem "The Wood Pile," the speaker chooses to walk out into the swamp with deeply divided feelings: "I will turn back from here. / No, I will go on further." We can contrast Thoreau's effusive praise of the swamp, of which he says, "if it were proposed to me to dwell in the neighborhood of the most beautiful garden that ever human art contrived, or else in a Dismal Swamp, I should certainly decide for the swamp," with Frost's "frozen swamp." While walking in the swamp "one gray day," Frost's speaker chances across an abandoned pile of split wood stacked neatly, "four by four by eight," as if its order revealed some kind of reciprocity between natural material and human effort. Significantly, the pile is held up, framed as it were, between a "tree / Still growing" and a humanly fashioned "stake." Frost's speaker wonders, "I thought that only / Someone who lived in turning to fresh tasks / Could so forget his handiwork"; but such optimism, based on an assumption of indefatigable human energy in the face of a wilderness to be tamed and used, conceals the more likely but repressed explanation for why the "measured" pile has been left in the woods: the farmer has not turned to a fresh task; rather, he has died.

An even more ironic reading of this passage is that the fresh task—a task that awaits everyone—is for the farmer to die. Indeed, the ending of the poem offers us increasingly darkening ironies. The speaker is baffled as to why the farmer's effortful work, "the labor of his ax," should be spent in vain to leave the woodpile "far from a useful fireplace / To warm the frozen swamp as best it could / With the slow smokeless burning of decay." The decaying woodpile, of course, cannot warm the swamp, and the attentive reader can hear much sardonic bitterness in the phrase "as best it could." This is a pathetic "best," indicating Frost's belief in nature's dominance over humankind. From the perspective of Frost's wish for personal survival, the cycling of nature means destruction and decay, exactly the opposite of Wordsworth's vision of "the immeasurable height / Of woods decaying, never to be decayed," in which life is seen impersonally as emerging out of death.

To read this poem simply as a typical Frostian vision of "decay" that overrides "useful" human effort would be misleading. The very fact, grim though it is, that nature's power surpasses human power often is a source of awe and reverence for Frost, evoking a mysterious sense of beauty in such lines as "Far in the pillared dark / Thrush music went." Even in "Out! Out!," when a boy loses his hand and dies in a buzz-saw accident, the natural backdrop against which the human tragedy is enacted is described almost ecstatically: "And from there those that lifted eyes could count / Five mountain ranges one behind the other / Under the sunset far into Vermont."

On the other side of the visionary spectrum from seeing wilderness as a challenge to human survival, one finds Frost's optimistic poem "Two Look at Two," in which the lovers can understand their bond to each other only within the context of their bond to nature, as exemplified by the deer across the wall who mirror their own desires and creaturehood. Frost ends his poem with the lovers looking at the deer, and thus seeing themselves, with a tidal upsurge of feeling, as part of the unity of the natural world:

> Still they stood,
> A great wave from it going over them,

As if the earth in one unlooked-for favor
Had made them certain earth returned their love.

In response to Emerson's statement that passion makes "nature grow conscious," Frost replied: "There is such a thing as getting too transcended. There are limits." The happy paradox of "Two Look at Two" is that the lovers achieve their feeling of transcendence only when they realize the earth-bound limits of their natural bodies.

The need to impose human order on nature is wittily expressed in Wallace Stevens's famous little poem "Anecdote of the Jar," in which the speaker, as prototypical poet, places a jar on a hill in the Tennessee landscape. The effect of this artistic placement of the jar is to make "the slovenly wilderness / Surround that hill." The jar does not partake of the plenitude of the wilderness since it does "not give of bird or bush," though by organizing them pictorially, according to an aesthetic principle, the jar "took dominion everywhere." This playful poem differs, however, from Stevens's fundamentally Heraclitean view of nature as flux—a view quite similar to Frost's vision of the decaying swamp.

For Stevens, paradoxically, change is the only universal constant. In his "The Auroras of Autumn," the aging speaker is walking along a deserted beach, deeply aware of his own finitude in relation to the stars and the effulgent night sky; he virtually sees himself disappearing when he says: "Here, being visible is being white." When he looks up at the streaming lights, however, he has a vision of the universe as a theater of change. This cosmic spectacle, for which he is the audience, is extremely beautiful; though totally indifferent to him, yet it is as if the universe enjoys being observed, as if human consciousness were the means by which the universe could contemplate itself:

> It is a theater floating through the clouds,
> Itself a cloud, although of misted rock
> And mountains running like water, wave on wave,
>
> Through waves of light. It is of cloud transformed
> To cloud transformed again, idly, the way
> A season changes color to no end,
>
> Except the lavishing of itself in change,
> As light changes yellow into gold and gold
> To its opal elements and fire's delight,
>
> Splashed wide-wise because it likes magnificence
> And the solemn pleasures of magnificent space.

The lavishness and lushness of Stevens's language, built of incremental repetitions and variations of phrases, conveys the speaker's sensuous delight in the act of looking. To be a spectator of this cosmic theater—even though the changes it makes manifest will obliterate the rapt observer, since he too is part of the spectacle of change—is to partake of nature's universal beauty. The dread of annihilation, for this moment, is absorbed in the impersonal grandeur of the spectacle, the dominion nature takes over any human being who contemplates its endless transformations.

It is not enough for Stevens, however, to lose himself in a sublime instant of aesthetic observation; he must force his vision of change to include the awareness of his own annihilation and then force this awareness to include the annihilation even of awareness. This is the extreme to which he attempts to extend consciousness when, in response to his vision of the night sky as a "theater" of change, he exclaims:

> This is nothing until in a single man contained,
> Nothing until this named thing nameless is
> And is destroyed.

The naming mind must contain its own destruction, its own unnaming, its own resulting namelessness, and in doing so, the imagination must experience nature in the aspect of nothingness. There is, of course, an element of what I will call "cosmic dread" in such a vision, and Stevens articulates this basic emotion in comparing the little light of his own life with the vastness of the Northern Lights when he says, "The scholar of one candle sees / An Arctic effulgence flaring on the frame / Of everything he is. And he feels afraid." This fear, this awareness of nature's dominating power, makes possible the poet's apprehension of beauty in the extreme and gives to the moment of mortal consciousness its precious poignance.

In William Carlos Williams also, the awareness of annihilating change intensifies and gives focus to thought. But nature's destructiveness, for Williams, has been vastly enhanced through human technology. Now that the atomic bomb, in particular, has enlarged our powers of destruction, human consciousness never again can be the same: "the bomb / has entered our lives / to destroy us. Every drill / driven into the earth / for oil enters my side / also," Williams Carlos Williams claims in "Asphodel, That Greeny Flower." In "The Orchestra," Williams addresses the issue of the radical change in the history of humankind's relationship to nature. In a prose passage inserted to interrupt Williams's normal poetic stanza, the step-down tercet, he asserts: "Man has survived hitherto because he was too ignorant to know how to realize his wishes. Now that he can realize them, he must either change them or perish." The wishes that Williams alludes to here might be interpreted simply as inherent human destructiveness that inevitably turns against itself, perhaps out of guilt or the awareness of original sin. Such wishes might well be driven by an instinct for death, the Freudian thanatos. Or these wishes might be seen as synonymous with the desire for domination, the wish to become like gods, which, when thwarted by nature's demand that we must die, are perverted into the blind wish to destroy or the fatal attempt of civilization to subdue nature. In any case, what Williams asks of our species is no less than a total change of heart, an act of will that would enable us to reinvent human psychology. Williams calls the fatal wish for domination the "wrong note," and the implication of his carefully chosen musical metaphor is that human beings have evolved to threaten nature's fundamental harmony. The poem's opening comparison between birdcalls at dawn and the tuning up of a human orchestra establishes the idea of the interdependence of the fate of human beings and of nature:

> The precise counterpart
>   of a cacophony of bird calls
>   lifting the sun almighty
> into his sphere: wood-winds
>   clarinet and violins
>   sound a prolonged A!

Ultimately, the triumph of the human wish for domination, if we are to survive, must take the form of human beings taking dominion over their own wish to dominate, taking dominion not over nature but over themselves. Williams continues to develop this theme of self-mastery by expanding the analogy between self-control and musical or poetic artistry: "it is a principle of music / to repeat the theme. / Repeat and repeat again, / as the pace mounts. The / theme is difficult / but no more difficult / than the facts [of human destructiveness] to be / resolved." The final lines of the poem celebrate the human capacity for resolving the danger we have created for ourselves by redesigning our own nature—a nature in which we are linked as fellow creatures to the birds and yet set apart in having to make the paradoxical choice not to set ourselves apart:

> The birds twitter now anew
>   but a design
>   surmounts their twittering.
> It is a design of a man
>   that makes them twitter.
>   It is a design.

VI

In addressing the issue of the need for a new philosophy of nature that could support the new environmentalism, Nash argues for a fundamental shift from human arrogance, based on the assumption that the earth was created for human exploitation, to an attitude of humility, of respect for the earth as something valuable in its own right: "The lesson most frequently drawn from both ecology and wilderness was the need for humility on the part of man." This humility would allow human-kind to adopt a philosophy of restraint, of accepting limits: "Preserving wilderness means establishing limits. We say, in effect, we will go this far, and no farther, for development. We agree to do without the material resources the wilderness might contain." The word *humility* is well chosen, for it derives from the Latin *humilis*, literally meaning of the ground or, by practice, to cover oneself with dirt, a gesture that reminds us of both our origins and the fate we share with all other creatures on planet Earth.

The ecological writers I have selected here for their passion and persuasiveness as exemplifying this new morality of setting limits are Rachel Carson and Bill McKibben. The approach these writers take is to reinforce their philosophical positions with scientific evidence that demonstrates what the catastrophic effects will be to the planet and to our health, both physical and spiritual, should our species not radically alter its self-indulgent ways.

In 1962, with the publication of *Silent Spring*, Rachel Carson sounded her heroic cry in defense of protecting the American landscape from the chemical assault directed against it. She begins by arguing that an unprecedented and unforeseen danger to the earth has appeared on the evolutionary scene: "Only within the moment of time represented by the present century has one species—man—acquired significant power to alter the nature of the world." This means that the earliest human wish to take dominion now can be realized through human technology. In evolutionary terms, human technological power belongs in the same category as other catastrophes (what David M. Raup, in *Extinction*, calls "first-strike" scenarios), like the demise of the dinosaurs due to the crashing of a comet into the earth. What the devastating comet or aster-oid was to the dinosaurs—who, of course, had insufficient time to adapt to the suddenly changed atmosphere—are we human beings to mam-malian and forest life today. But with this difference: the dinosaurs were not the agents of their own destruction, as we are likely to be of our own demise. Shakespeare expresses his insight into the consequences of the human greed for possession and exploitation when he says: "And appetite, an universal wolf, at last eats up itself."

Carson emphasizes the evolutionary origin of both the planet and our species, one among many: "It took hundreds of millions of years to produce the life that now inhabits the earth—eons of time in which that developing and evolving and diversifying life reached a state of ad-justment and balance with its surroundings." And she points out that what is new in environmental terms is the *rate of change* brought about by technological intervention. This difference in degree in the speed of environmental change completely alters the capacity of the whole ecological system to keep itself in balance: "The rapidity of change and the speed with which new situations are created follow the impetuous and heedless pace of man rather than the deliberate pace of nature."

Human beings, themselves the products of gradual evolutionary changes, are not designed to comprehend the consequences human culture and human reproduction have wrought upon the earth. (As Robert Ornstein argues in *New World, New Mind*: "Cultural evolution, in only a few generations, has made the size of the human population a threat to the survival of civilization. The gene pool cannot respond to that threat at all; for individuals to lower their reproductive output goes against the basic rules of biological evolution.") Since we are not gods, we have great difficulty in addressing ourselves to any long-range vision of the future. Carson argues that "we have allowed these chemicals, as with other human indulgences, to be used with little or no advance investigation of their effect on soil, water, wildlife, and man himself."

Just as Carson offers numerous examples and details about the chemical pollution of our environment and ourselves, so too Bill McKibben offers statistics to prove that "we have substantially altered the earth's atmosphere." He details the various possible consequences of the "greenhouse effect" and points out that just "an increase of 1 degree in average temperature moves the climatic zones thirty-five to fifty miles north." The next round of consequences that will follow is that trees will die, releasing further "staggering amounts of carbon into the atmosphere," and inevitably—a future we refuse to foresee—"reproductive failure and forest die-back is estimated to begin between 2000 and 2050." McKibben's analytic prose rises to passionate imploration when he exclaims: "The trees will die. Consider nothing more than that—just that the trees will die."

At the heart of McKibben's analytical approach to environmental dangers lies an aesthetic and philosophical appeal to what, he believes, constitutes our essential humanity. To destroy nature, for McKibben, is to remove the primary model—a model of structural coherence that encompasses diversity—upon which our cultural sense of beauty is founded. McKibben perceives a profound sadness lurking beneath the noise and rush of modern society, which "is almost an aesthetic response—appropriate because we have marred a great, mad, profligate work of art, taken a hammer to the most perfectly proportioned of sculptures." He envisions that the loss of nature will result also in the loss of beauty and of meaning.

McKibben's judicious pessimism, however, leaves him room to say that "I hope against hope," and this hope is based on an appeal to reason that he considers to be natural to our species. "As birds have flight, our special gift is reason," McKibben declares, yet he reminds us that our reason is antithetical to the "biological imperatives toward endless growth in numbers and territory," the unconscious forces beneath the Biblical morality of taking dominion, the imperative to "Be fruitful and multiply." With visionary (but perhaps desperate) hopefulness, McKibben says: "We could exercise our reason to do what no other animal can do: we could limit ourselves voluntarily, choose to remain God's creatures instead of making ourselves gods."

Whether one believes literally in God or not, McKibben's meaning is clear, and, to my mind, it corresponds to the moral implicit in the biblical account of God's punishment of Adam because he rebelled against his bond to nature by seeking to become immortal. God sends Adam forth from the garden of Eden "lest he put forth his hand, and take also of the tree of life and live for ever." In taking dominion over the planet Earth, human beings, of course, have not mastered the universe nor taken dominion over the Second Law of Thermodynamics nor, most significantly of all, achieved eternal life that would set the human species apart from the fate of all of the other creatures that have walked upon the face of the earth.

With the first human awareness of death as an ongoing state of nonbeing, the desperate wish not to die must simultaneously have been born, as is implied, for example, in the earliest burial sites, in which possessions are placed in the grave to be taken with one on a journey. But taking dominion cannot mean that we can possess our bodies for long or that the Yeatsian wish, "Once out of nature I shall never take my bodily form from any natural thing," can ever be realized, except as a fantasy of artistic power that enables one to give birth to oneself—the artistic power that Prospero renounces at the end of *The Tempest*. No, taking dominion over nature can mean for our species only that we will have proved that our particular genius has been the destruction of many wondrous living forms but mainly destruction of ourselves. No doubt, the insects will survive our folly or some more adaptable life form will emerge in another solar system. To choose to remain creatures, then, as McKibben proposes, is to accept limits—the limits of mortality, the limits of power and possession—and thus to remember and remain true to our evolutionary origins.

Without a sense of beauty that derives from an awareness of others, from the realization that we are merely creatures in an evolving world that we share with other creatures, a prior world on which our fabricated cultural world depends, the capacity for taking delight in our surroundings will wither away. Even before the planet becomes inhospitable to the human species, we will have died in spirit, though perhaps superintelligent creatures of our own technological creation, based not on carbon but on silicon molecules, who do not depend on food or air or space or a moderate climate or leisure time for contemplating the good fortune of chance existence, will evolve to survive us in a state of happiness that we, still the children of nature, have not evolved to comprehend.

CONTRIBUTORS

SANDRA ALCOSSER's previous books include *A Fish to Feed All Hunger*.

PAMELA ALEXANDER is the author of *Commonwealth of Wings* and *Navigable Waterways*, which won the Yale Younger Poets Award in 1985.

JULIA ALVAREZ published her first book of poetry, *Homecoming*, in 1986; her novel, *How the Garcia Girls Lost Their Accents*, was published in 1991.

A. R. AMMONS's two latest books are *The Really Short Poems of A. R. Ammons* and *Sumerian Vistas*.

DAVID BAKER's last two books are *Sweet Home, Saturday Night*, and *Haunts*.

PETER BALAKIAN's two most recent books are *Theodore Roethke's Far Fields* and *Reply from Wilderness Island*.

MARVIN BELL's most recent work was *Iris of Creation*; he has a forthcoming book of poems, *The Book of the Dead Man*.

STEPHEN BERG is an editor of the *American Poetry Review* and the author, most recently, of *New and Selected Poems* (1992).

WENDELL BERRY is a well-known poet, novelist, and essayist whose books include his *Selected Poems*. He lives in Kentucky on a farm.

MICHAEL BLUMENTHAL teaches at Harvard and has published several volumes of poetry and has edited an anthology of love poems.

PHILIP BOOTH's most recent books include *Selves* and *Relations*.

CHRISTOPHER BUCKLEY has published many collections of verse, including *Blue Autumn*. He has edited a volume of criticism on the poetry of Philip Levine.

TERESA CADER is the author of *Guests* and the forthcoming *Sumerian Symbol for Bird*.

AMY CLAMPITT has recently published *Westward*, a book of poems, and *Predecessors, Et Cetera*, a book of essays.

JUDITH ORTIZ COFER's work includes *Silent Dancing* and a forthcoming book, *The Latin Deli*, which includes prose, fiction, and poetry.

MICHAEL COLLIER's two books of poetry are *The Clasp and Other Poems* and *The Folded Heart*.

CHARD DENIORD is the author of *Asleep in the Fire* and the forthcoming *Error at the Heart of Desire*.

CARL DENNIS's two most recent books of poetry are *Meetings with Time* and *The Outskirts of Troy*.

RITA DOVE's latest work includes a book of poetry, *Grace Notes*, and *Through the Ivory Gate*, a novel. She has won a Pulitzer Prize for her poetry.

CORNELIUS EADY is a widely published poet.

JOHN ENGELS is the author of *Cardinals in the Ice Age* and *Walking in Cootehill: New and Selected Poems, 1958–1992*.

CAROL FROST's two latest books are *Chimera* and *Day of the Body*.

ALICE FULTON's most recent books are *Powers of Congress* and *Palladium*.

DANA GIOIA has published several volumes of poetry, including *Daily Horoscope*, and a book of critical essays called *Can Poetry Matter?*

PAMELA WHITE HADAS has written a book on Marianne Moore and several volumes of poetry, including *Designing Women* and *Beside Herself*.

DONALD HALL's most recent books are *Their Ancient Glittering Eyes* and *The Museum of Clear Ideas*.

DANIEL HALPERN is editor of *Antaeus* and the author of numerous books of poetry.

JOY HARJO has written a chapbook, *The Last Song. Secrets from the Center of the World*, and several books of poetry, including *In Mad Love and War* and *What Moon Drove Me to This?*

JUAN FELIPE HERRERA's most recent books are *Facegames* and *Akrilica.*

WILLIAM HEYEN's two latest books are *Ribbons: The Gulf War*, and *Pterodactyl Rose: Poems of Ecology.*

EDWARD HIRSCH's latest work includes *The Night Parade* and *Wild Gratitude.*

ROALD HOFFMAN's recent books include *Gaps and Verges.*

JONATHAN HOLDEN's two latest books are a volume of poems, *American Gothic*, and a novel, *Brilliant Kids.*

GARRETT KAORU HONGO directs the writing program at the University of Oregon and has published several books of poetry.

DAVID HUDDLE's most recent work includes a book of poems, *The Nature of Yearning*, and *The Writing Habit: Essays.*

RICHARD JACKSON's two most recent books are *Alive All Day*, a collection of poems, and *Four Slovene Poets*, which he edited.

MARK JARMAN's two latest books are *Iris* and *The Black Riviera.*

DONALD JUSTICE's two most recent books are *The Sunset Maker* and *A Donald Justice Reader.*

RICHARD KENNEY is the author of *The Evolution of the Flightless Bird* and *Orrery.* He is the recipient of a MacArthur Fellowship.

MAXINE KUMIN recent publications include *Looking for Luck* and *Nuture.*

SYDNEY LEA's latest books are *The Blainville Testament* and *Prayer for the Little City.*

DAVID LEHMAN's work includes *Operation Memory*, a book of poems, and *Signs of the Times: Deconstruction and the Fall of Paul de Man.*

GARY MARGOLIS is the author of *The Day We Still Stand Here* and *Falling Awake.*

PAUL MARIANI's last two books are *Salvage Operations: New and Selected Poems*, and *Dream Song: The Life of John Berryman.*

CHARLES MARTIN's most recent works are *Steal the Bacon* and *Catullus.*

WILLIAM MATTHEWS's body of work includes, most recently, *Selected Poems and Translations*, and a book of essays, *Curiosities.*

J. D. MCCLATCHY's most recent books are a collection of poems, *The Rest of the Way*, and a translation of Horace's *Art of Poetry.* He is editor of *The Yale Review.*

CHRISTOPHER MERRILL has written several books of poetry and edited a volume of nature poetry.

JOHN FREDERICK NIMS's two most recent books are *The Six-Cornered Snowflake and Other Poems* and *Zany in Denim*.

JEAN NORDHAUS's last books are *A Bracelet of Lies* and *My Life in Hiding*.

CAROLE SIMMONS OLES is the author of *The Deed*.

GREGORY ORR teaches at the University of Virginia and has published several collections of poems, including *The Red House* and *We Must Make a Kingdom of It*.

ROBERT PACK's two most recent books are *The Long View*, a collection of essays, and a book of poems, *Before it Vanishes*.

JAY PARINI's latest books are *Bay of Arrows* and *The Last Station*.

LINDA PASTAN's last two books were *The Imperfect Paradise* and *Heroes in Disguise*.

ROBERT PINSKY's two most recent books are *The Want Bone* and *Poetry and the World*.

STANLEY PLUMLY's books include *Out-of-the-Body Travel* and *Celestial Summer*.

WYATT PRUNTY has published several volumes of poetry and a book on modern and contemporary poetry. He teaches at the University of the South and directs the Sewanee Writers' Conference.

HILDA RAZ's latest books of poetry are *What Is Good* and *The Bone Dish*.

IRA SADOFF's last two books are *An Ira Sadoff Reader* and *Emotional Traffic*.

SHEROD SANTOS's last book was *The Southern Reaches*; *The City of Women* is forthcoming.

JANE SHORE's last two books were *Eye Level* and *The Minute Hand*.

ROBERT SIEGEL's two most recent books are *In a Pig's Eye* and *White Whale*.

TOM SLEIGH is the author of two books of poetry, *After One* and *Waking*.

DAVE SMITH edits *The Southern Review*. His numerous volumes of poetry include *Cuba Nights* and *The Roundhouse Voices*.

GARY SNYDER's most recent book is a volume of new and selected poems called *No Nature*.

KATHERINE SONIAT's previous works include *A Shared Life*, which was recently selected for the Iowa Poetry Prize (Edwin Ford Piper Award).

MARCIA SOUTHWICK is the author of two books, *The Night Won't Save Anyone* and *Why the River Disappears*.

WILLIAM STAFFORD's recent work includes *Passwords* and *The Animal that Drank Up Sound*.

GERALD STERN's most recent books are *Leaving Another Kingdom: Selected Poems*, and *Bread Without Sugar*.

ANNE STEVENSON's two latest books of poetry are *Selected Poems* and *The Other House*. She has also written a biography of Sylvia Plath.

MARK STRAND's recent books are *The Continuous Life* and *Dark Harbour*. He is a recent Poet Laureate of the United States.

DABNEY STUART's latest works are *Sweet Lucy Wine*, a collection of stories, and *Narcissus Dreaming*, a book of poems.

ERIC TRETHEWEY has published several collections of poetry.

CHASE TWICHELL's two most recent books are *Perdido* and *The Practice of Poetry: Writing Exercises from Poets who Teach*.

MONA VAN DUYN's works include *If It Be Not I: Collected Poems, 1959–1983*, and the forthcoming book of poems *Firefall*. She recently won a Pulitzer Prize for Poetry.

MARILYN NELSON WANIEK's two most recent books are *Mama's Promises* and *The Homeplace*.

ROSANNA WARREN's most recent books of poetry are *Stained Glass* and *Each Leaf Shines Separate*.

RICHARD WILBUR's most recent works are *More Opposites* and *School for Husbands*, a translation from Molière. He is a recent Poet Laureate of the United States.

NANCY WILLARD's latest books are *A Nancy Willard Reader* and *Sister Water*.

CHARLES WRIGHT's two most recent books are *Country Music* (second edition), and *The World of the Ten Thousand Things*.

GARY YOUNG's last two books are *The Dream of a Moral Life* and *Nine Days: New York*.

PAUL ZIMMER's latest works include *The Great Bird of Love* and *Family Reunion: Selected and New Poems*.

ACKNOWLEDGMENTS

The editors would like to thank the following publications and publishers for the use of previously published poems, some of which appeared in a different form:

Adirondack Life, The American Poetry Review, The American Voice, The Amicus Journal, Antioch Review, ATLATL, Beliot Poetry Journal, Black Warrior Review, The Blue Mesa Review, The Bluffs Reader, The Boston Review, Boulevard, The Cambridge Review, The Christian Science Monitor, Colorado Review, Crazyhorse, Cream City Review, The Denver Quarterly, The Desert News, Field, The Georgia Review, Gettysburg Review, The Iron Mountain Review, The Johns Hopkins University Press, *The Journal, Louisville Review, Manoa, Michigan Quarterly Review, The Missouri Review, The Nation, Negative Capability, The New Criterion, New England Review, New Virginia Review, The New Yorker, Nimrod, The North American Review, North Dakota Quarterly, Northern Lights, Ohio Review, Paris Review, Partisan Review, Phoebe, Ploughshares, Poetry, Poetry East, The Poetry Miscellany, Poetry Northwest, Prairie Schooner, Quarterly West, The Seasons in Vermont, Sewanee Theological Review, The Southeast Review, Southern Review, Sun Dog, Tar River Poetry, Threepenny Review, TriQuarterly, Verse, Virginia Quarterly Review, The Voice Literary Supplement* (December 1991), *Western Humanities Review, Wilderness, Willow Springs, Window, Women's Review of Books,* and *The Yale Review.*

UNIVERSITY PRESS OF NEW ENGLAND
publishes books under its own imprint and is the publisher for Brandeis University Press, Brown University Press, University of Connecticut, Dartmouth College, Middlebury College Press, University of New Hampshire, University of Rhode Island, Tufts University, University of Vermont, and Wesleyan University Press.

Library of Congress Cataloging-in-Publication Data

Poems for a small planet : contemporary American nature poetry / edited by Robert Pack and Jay Parini.
   p.   cm. — (A Bread loaf anthology)
ISBN 0–87451–620–X. — ISBN 0–87451–621–8 (pbk.)
   1. Nature—Poetry.   2. American poetry—20th century.   I. Pack, Robert, 1929–
II. Parini, Jay.   III. Series.
PS595.N22P63   1993
811'.5408036—dc20   92–56909